RELIEF IS GREATLY WANTED

The Battle of Fort William Henry

The enemy are constantly playing upon us from two batteries of nine pieces of cannon each. Relief is greatly wanted.

—Lt. Col. George Monro
to Maj. Gen. Webb, August 8, 1757

Edward J. Dodge

HERITAGE BOOKS
2007

HERITAGE BOOKS
AN IMPRINT OF HERITAGE BOOKS, INC.

Books, CDs, and more—Worldwide

For our listing of thousands of titles see our website
at
www.HeritageBooks.com

Published 2007 by
HERITAGE BOOKS, INC.
Publishing Division
65 East Main Street
Westminster, Maryland 21157-5026

Copyright © 1998 Edward J. Dodge

Cover illustration and Ranger illustrations on pp. 178-182
by Clyde A. Risley
Maps on pp. 139-143 and drawings on p. 20 and p. 33
rendered by Nick Ackermann

All rights reserved. No part of this book may be reproduced or transmitted in any form or by any means, electronic or mechanical, including photocopying, recording or by any information storage and retrieval system without written permission from the author, except for the inclusion of brief quotations in a review.

International Standard Book Number: 978-0-7884-0932-8

Dedication

*To the memory of Sharon Tracy Cole.
May you always have the warm sun to your face
and a fair breeze to your back.*

Table Of Contents

Dedication iii
List Of Illustrations vi
Acknowledgments vii
Foreword ix
1. Prelude 1
2. Pressure Leads To Rupture 5
3. A Humiliation Of Arms 13
4. Beginning Of The End 19
5. Preliminaries 31
6. The First Go Round 39
7. A Time Of Peace 47
8. Six Days Of Purgatory 55
9. Capture Was Worse Than Death 87
10. A Day In Hell 89
11. Too Late For Too Many 95
12. Aftermath 99
13. Final Chapter 125
14. Postscript 131
15. Epilogue 145
16. His Majesty's Independent Company Of Rangers .. 161
Ranger Uniform Illustrations by Clyde A. Risley ... 177
About the Author 185
Bibliography 187
Index 193

LIST OF ILLUSTRATIONS

1. Map of French, Indian and English Borderlands, 1756-64.. xii-xiii
2. The Portage between Lake George and Lake Champlain 3
3. Geometrical Plan of Fort Edward and Environs, 1756 18
4. Fort St. Frederic (Crown Point) 20
5. A Plan of the Town and Fort of Carillon
   at Ticonderoga, July 1758 22
6. Bloody Pond 26
7. Photograph of the reconstructed Fort William Henry 29
8. Plan of Fort William Henry, 1756 33
9. Fort William Henry: Corner of fort headquarters 34
10. Fort William Henry: Headquarters and hospital building 35
11. Louis-Joseph, Marquis de Montcalm. 49
12. Memo from Monro concerning strength of
    Fort William Henry at time of August 1757 attack 54
13. Monro's letter, "Relief is greatly wanted." 73
14. Return of the Killed, Wounded and Missing,
    dated 25 August 1757 96
15. Roster of Officers of 1st Battalion, 62nd Regiment of Foot,
    or Royal Americans (Later the 60th Royal Americans) 118
16. Roster of Officers of the Royal Americans 119
17. Monthly Return dated 25 November 1757 with notation of
    Col. Monro's death 120
18. Monthly Return dated 25 December 1757 with notation of
    Col. Monro's death 121
19. Lt. Col. Monro's Petition for Retirement as a Physician 122
20. Fort Anne Blockhouse, Present Day Bank Building 135
21. Fort Ticonderoga. Upper and lower defense positions 136
22. Fort Ticonderoga. Defensive inner wall 137
23. Fort Ticonderoga. Drawbridge to demi-lune 138

24. Key to Map figures for Driving Tour 139
25. Map 1: Lake George at Fort William Henry 140
26. Map 2. Lake George, central section, Sabbath Day Point 141
27. Map 3. Lake George at Ticonderoga 142
28. Map 4. Lake Champlain at Crown Point, (Fort St. Frederic) ... 143
29. Major-General John Burgoyne 153
30. Major Robert Rogers 160
31. Rogers' Rangers Muster Roll for
    23 July 1756 to 27 September 1756 167
32. Muster Roll of Rogers' Rangers
    Officers of the 12 Ranger Companies 168
33. Muster Roll of Rogers' Rangers
    Officers of the 12 Ranger Companies - Corrections 169
34. Church where Robert Rogers was buried 176
35. Rangers illustrated by Clyde A. Risley 178
36. Grave marker for Lt. Col. George Monro 184
37. The author and others at dedication ceremony
    for Monro's grave marker 185

Acknowledgments

This book would never have been written without the help and support of Major (Retired) Alan and June Harfield; Allen and Mary Lu Metz; Carole Tracy; Major (Retired) John Ainsworth, Royal Sussex Regimental Association; Brian Driscoll, Archivist, National Archives of Canada; Colonel (Retired) John Francis, Queen's Regiment; Duke of Montrose, Natal, South Africa; James Monroe, Leesburg, Virginia; Keith Monroe, Miskayama, New York; Captain (Retired) Patrick Monroe, Evanton, Dingwall, Scotland; Miss Elizabeth Talbot (Retired), National Army Museum; S. C. Humphrey, Southwark Arts Libraries and Entertainments; Dr. and Mrs. Peter Boyden, National Army Museum; John Stark, Newton, Massachusetts; Michael Wycznski, Archivist, National Archives of Canada; Mrs. Judith Rust, St. Mary Newington Church; Paul Lemieux, Archivist, National Archives, Canada; Timothy Dube, Archivist, National Archives, Canada; Karen E. Kearns and Dan Lewis, The Huntington Library, San Marino, California; William F. Imrie, Burnt Hills, New York; Clyde A. Risley, Charlton, New York; Robert Flacke, Sr., President-Fort William Henry Corporation, Lake George, New York; Michael Palumbo, Curator - Fort William Henry, Lake George, New York; Emily Edwards, Springfield, Illinois; Steve Ritchie and Tom Stevens, Photo Resource Center, Springfield, Illinois; Ken Oglesby, Flag World, Springfield, Illinois; and my wife Ann for putting up with the mess and clutter.

Foreword

In the supplement to the *New York Mercury* of August 1, 1757, there appeared a letter from an unidentified writer dated July 26, 1757. It tells of the ambush of Colonel John Parker's 350-man waterborne scout. It relates in a somewhat vague fashion the number of men killed, with specifics as to officers. It does mention one sergeant who survived, but not by name. In closing, the writer cannot understand what all the enemy are doing in the area.

On August 6, 1757, a letter was written from G. W. Banyar, Deputy Secretary to His Honor the Lieutenant Governor, to the colonels commanding the militia in the counties of Westchester and Queens; that having been advised by Major General Webb that Fort William Henry was under attack by a large body of the enemy, the militia in the counties mentioned should hold in readiness 400 able-bodied and effective men.

His Majesty's Council in the city of New York sent a letter dated August 13, 1757, to the colonel commanding the militia of Queens and Suffolk Counties advising that 600 men from Queens County were to be sent to Albany to preserve that city. It further stated that they had been advised by express that both Fort William Henry and Fort Edward had been attacked and taken by the enemy.

The Council of New York sent a letter dated August 14, 1757, to the Honorable James DeLancey, Lieutenant Governor in Albany, stating they had received his letter of the 11th instant advising that Fort Edward was not under attack and glad to hear that the affair at Fort William Henry was not as bad as first appeared.

On August 15, 1757, Richard Floyd, who was apparently the colonel commanding the Suffolk County militia, wrote to

His Majesty's Council of the City of New York relating that the Suffolk County militia was on its way to Westchester. However, due to a poor state of health, he would not be marching with it.

Finally, on August 22, 1757, an article appeared in the *New York Mercury* reporting that on the 12th instant an express from Albany arrived advising of the surrender of Fort William Henry to a large army of French. The same day (the 12th), 700 volunteers from New York turned out and the next day left for Albany.

Time, distance, too few – too late, questionable leadership, an unwieldy chain of command, faulty communication and confusion. This, then, was the dichotomy of the French and Indian War.

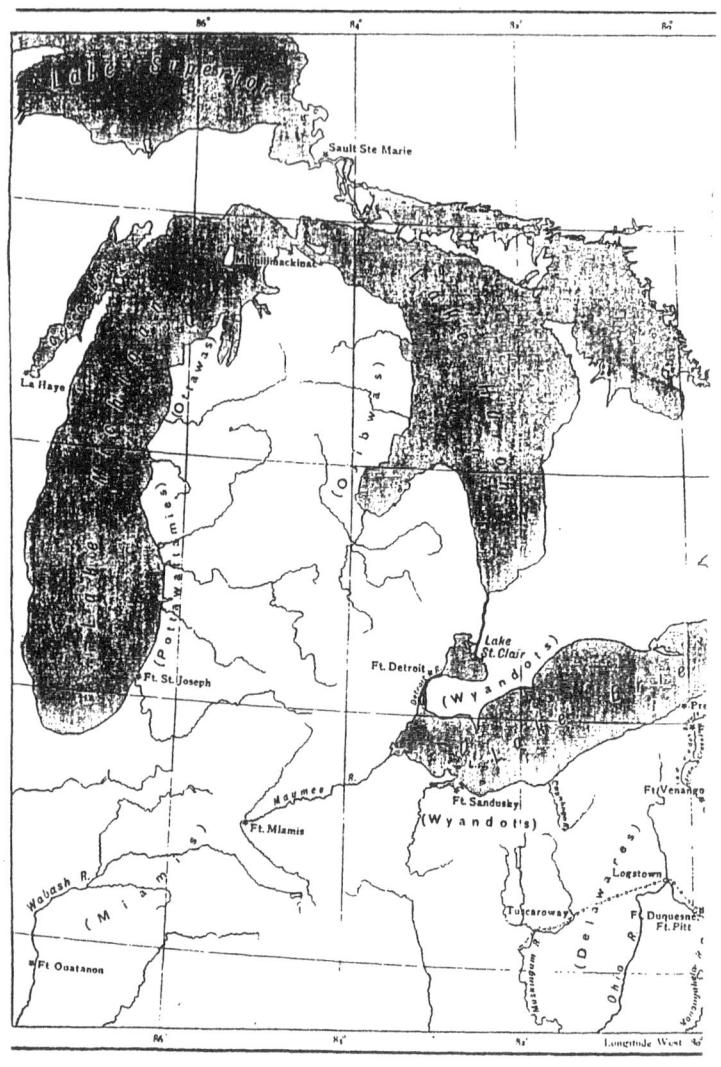

Map of French, Indian and English Borderlands, 1756-64.

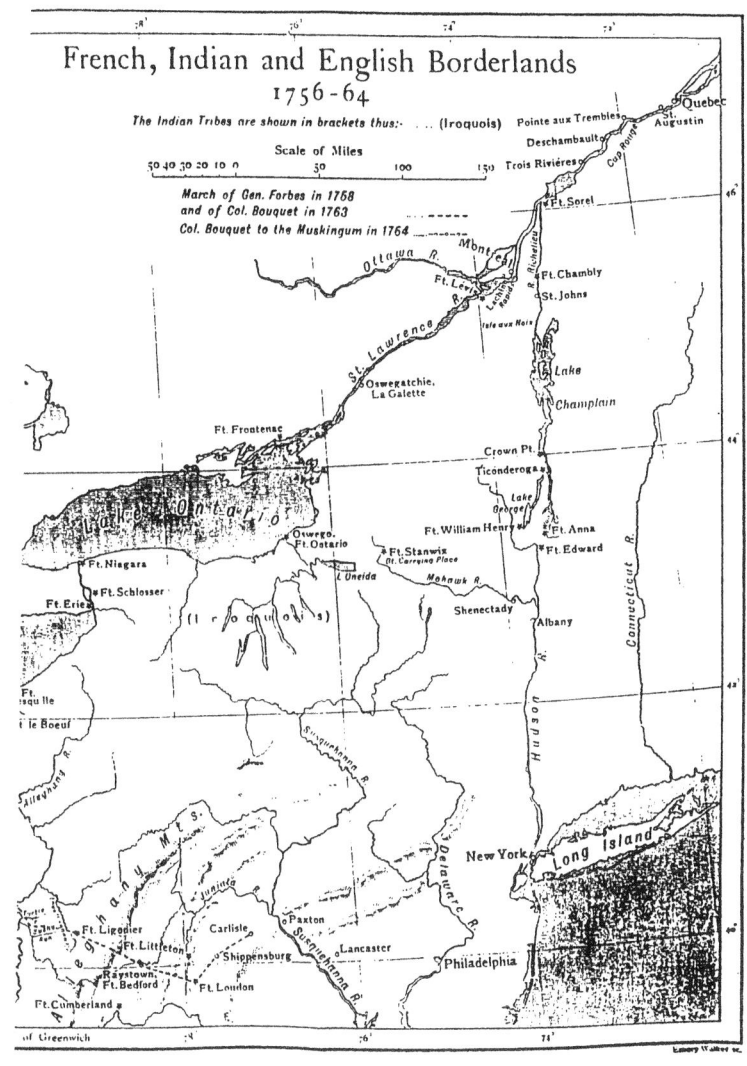

Published by kind permission of the Council of The Society for Army Historical Research, London, England.

Chapter One

PRELUDE

1700.... In Europe, power struggles were germinating which would change the world. Wars ebbed and flowed with no real winners, prompting the start of still more wars, which would extend to the new world – North America.

In North America, the seeds of conflict had already been sown over the past 91 years. This conflict would involve Europeans, colonists of the New World and the natives of that continent in what would become the most savage war yet known to man. It would have no equal for another 200 years. France and England were both in North America, with France already embroiled in the conflict and Britain slowly being sucked into the vacuum. The conflict would last for 154 years and would cost both nations in money and human life a figure never to be accurately known. It would create a rift between the natives and the newcomers that is smoldering even now, 230 years later.

That same year a lad of Scottish blood was born in Ireland. Twelve years later a lad of French blood would be born. They knew nothing of each other and would have passed on the road with little more than a nod. But in 1757 they would meet in a foreign land; the older because he was ordered there, the younger because he wanted to be there. The meeting place: Fort William Henry, Lake George, New York, North America.

Lake George, New York, is one of nature's most spectacular works. A spring-fed lake lying in a glacial trough, it is 32 miles long and one to three miles in width, with 109 miles of shoreline. It is 195 feet at its greatest depth. Within its 44 square miles are 300 islands. It is located in the Adirondacks and has mountains to the east and west.

The Adirondacks comprise the oldest mountain range in North America. They are not exceedingly high, averaging in this area some 2,200 feet on the west side of the lake and 2,600 feet on the east side. The slopes are cut with ravines and crevasses deceptively covered by underbrush and low growth. Tree cover is thick, close and multi-specied. Open areas are sheer cliffs of granite or inclines of incredible angle, merging from and into glades and meadows. Low spots become bogs, marshes and swamps inhabited by rattlesnakes, leeches, ticks, deer flies, black flies, gnats and mosquitoes. The rivers are many, varying from wide, navigable boatways to small deep whitewater courses through impassible cliffs and forests. Varied wildlife, game birds and fish abound in the area.

Lake George has been referred to by many names. For a few years the British military called it simply one of the Little Lakes. It flows into Lake Champlain to the north and also has been called the Tail of Lake Champlain. It was called Andiatarocte by the Huron and Iroquois, Lac du St. Sacrement by the French, Iroquois Lake by the early British colonists and, finally, named in honor of his king by Sir William Johnson. James Fenimore Cooper stated it was also known as the Horican.

The lake is box-shaped on its southern shore. The area was a wide, sandy beach merging into the foot of a small bluff which rose some 50 feet above the lake. Fort William Henry was located on the bluff.

The fort was destined to become one of the focal points of the French and Indian War. During its short life it would serve as a depot for the 35th Regiment of Foot, 44th Regiment of Foot, elements of the 60th Regiment of Foot and His Majesty's Independent Company of Rangers, as well as militia units from Massachusetts, New Hampshire, Connecticut, New York, and New Jersey. Through its gates would pass many who would become famous. It was a military base, a place of shelter and camaraderie, and, for many, the only grave marker they would ever have.

The Portage between Lake George and Lake Champlain.

Chapter Two

PRESSURE LEADS TO RUPTURE

A young George Washington, who led a surprise attack against a French patrol unit in western Pennsylvania in 1755, has been credited with starting the French and Indian War. This is not true, nor was it ever even near truth. The war started in 1609.

The French and Indian War was truly a European conflict fought on North American soil. To fully understand it, a brief review of European wars of the 17th and 18th centuries is helpful.

The French and Indian War paralleled four European wars. The first was the War of the Grand Alliance, 1688-97. In the colonies it was known as King William's War and spanned the period 1689-97. In 1690 the English captured Port Royal in present-day Nova Scotia. They would lose it a year later.

Next was the War of Spanish Succession, known in the colonies as Queen Anne's War in the colonies. This war lasted from 1702-13. During this period, Deerfield, Massachusetts, was attacked (in 1704), a second attack was made on Port Royal (in 1710) and the English established fur-trading posts in Hudson's Bay area in the heart of Canada, or New France, as it was then called.

The third war, the War of Austrian Succession, was known as King George's War in the colonies, and spanned the years 1744-48. In the New World during this period, the French captured Fort Clinton at the site of present-day Saratoga Springs, New York.

The fourth conflict was known in Europe as the Seven Years' War, 1756-63. The colonists knew it as the French and Indian War, spanning the years 1754 to 1763. It was during this period that the worst fighting occurred in the colonies.

The reasons for the war have been given as empire building, English and Protestant versus French and Catholic, and the fur trade. All are valid to some extent. However, the European wars served to mask the real reason for involvement of New France and the colonies. Simply, Canada or New France was attempting to prevent a trade deficit being forced on it by Mother France. If France could control the fur trade which was Canada's bargaining power for needed supplies, then Canada would be in desperate straits. The problem was complex and in its complexity drew the English into the struggle in the new world.

By the early 1600's New France was beginning to plant its own roots. The government was still controlled by France, but as new generations were born, educated and came into positions of authority, Canadians started taking over the leadership of Canada, with France becoming a supportive extension to the native born. They looked to France for manpower, woman power, certain foodstuffs and equipment which they did not as yet have the facilities to manufacture. France was willing to supply these items, but continually sent individuals who were strong French nationalists and worked for France and not Canada, thus internal politics extended even to the church, where lay brothers and priests from the same orders worked against each other.

Even with the internal struggle, New France and France would fight side-by-side against what they felt was a common enemy, the English. New France needed to protect its source of marketable items and France to protect its investment in territorial expansion and a new, cheaper source of fur.

New France started compounding her problems as early as July of 1609. There were two major Indian or tribal confederations within her sphere of influence, Iroquois and Algonquin. Although the two spoke the same basic language, they were enemies. Sieur Samuel de Champlain was, at the time, exploring what would eventually become part of northern New York. He met and fell in with a part of the Algonquin nation, with whom the French were friendly.

As they proceeded south they came upon an Iroquois party and a battle took place. Champlain won the battle for the Algonquins. He fired his arquebus, killing two Iroquois and wounding a third. As a result of this act, the Iroquois harbored a hatred for the French that would continue for 150 years. It also provided a basis for future attacks against Canada by the Iroquois.

With the arrival of the English colonists in 1620 and the Dutch in 1626, the tide shifted against the French again. In their trade with the tribes, the English learned that firearms were prized, particularly by the Iroquois. With the possession of firearms, the Iroquois became even more aggressive. The raids against the Algonquins became more frequent and severe, and with them, attacks against the French became more aggressive. The Iroquois so devastated the Huron tribe that they became virtually extinct. The name "Iroquois," however, would be applied by the English to all tribes supported by or supportive of the French.

By 1687 the situation was intolerable in French eyes and the Marquis de Denonville, between 10 June and 6 July 1687 massed a force of 832 French, 930 Canadians, 800 Indians and 180 *coureurs de bois* and attacked the Senecas, who were part of the Iroquois nation. This resulted in a total destruction of the Seneca villages and an estimated 400 Seneca dead.

The tribal warfare abated and treaty talks were held in Montreal in June 1688. The talks rapidly fell apart and in August 1688 the Iroquois attacked the village of Lachine near Montreal. They burned 56 of the 77 homes, took 90 prisoners, killed 24 and roasted five children while Montreal watched. The Senecas had been avenged.

Finally, in January 1690, after receiving word of the conflict in Europe, the French made their first move against the English. Their logic was twofold: first, the English supported the Iroquois who had attacked Lachine; second, by creating havoc in the English plantations, they might be able to divert some of England's military from Europe to the New World.

The original plan called for an attack on Albany, New York. However, the weather in January is unpredictable at best in northern New York. January 1690 was no different. The attacking force of 210 combined Canadians and Indians found themselves cloaked in a sub-zero cold with a blizzard blowing. They changed the target of their strike to a small Dutch settlement, Schenectady, and attacked at 11 o'clock at night. The Dutch had not closed their gates nor mounted sentries due to the weather. A point of irony is the children of Schenectady had built two snowmen, one on either side of the gate, and these were the sentries that night. One report claims that the attack was accompanied by shouts of "Lachine – Lachine," which appears doubtful in view of the general weather conditions. Regardless, within minutes the 40 dwellings which composed the settlement were ablaze.

According to the few survivors who straggled into Albany early the following morning in their night clothes, and later confirmed by the few who were rescued from the attack party that was taking them to Canada, the Canadians stood by while the Hurons ran their course of torture and butchery.

The Albany newspaper quoted the mayor of Albany as stating in reference to the attack, "Ye women big with child, ripped up and down and ye children alive thrown into flames and their heads dashed in pieces against doors and windows."

In the spring of 1691, a thousand Iroquois attacked Montreal, Trois-Rivières and the settlements between the two. In the fall of 1691 the only attack by British colonists against Canada was made. Apparently a relief column had arrived in present-day Nova Scotia to assist the British at Port Royal. As it approached the settlement of La Prairie it was fired on by the members of the settlement. The English colonists suffered no killed or wounded, but the French Canadian settlement lost two men, four women killed and 19 taken prisoner. The government of New France used this incident to build up a story of multiple raids involving the most horrible of deeds, torture and butchery. There are, to this day, those who believe the latter.

In the spring of 1693, the French raided and wiped out five Mohawk villages in New York. In the chase column was Major Peter Schuyler of the Schuyler Patent, or what is now Saratoga Springs. The column finally caught up with the raiders near the site of Ticonderoga. A battle ensued, but the French escaped. A rest was taken by the column and as it was cold and wet, fires were started and food was cooked. Someone offered Schuyler a bowl of soup which he started to drink – until he saw a human hand floating in the broth. To the Indians on both sides, available food was available food.

After the 1704 raid on Deerfield, Massachusetts, in which 50 people were killed and many were taken captive, hostilities on the western and northern frontiers, as they were known, quieted down. Not all the energies of the French had been used up in warfare.

By 1687 the French, using the resourcefulness of such men as LaSalle, Joliet and Marquette, had explored the upper and western Great Lakes region, the Ohio River watershed and the Mississippi watershed from its source to the Gulf of Mexico. It was this area that the king of France claimed in the name of France and made LaSalle the governor-general.

Not until 1722, with the founding of New Orleans, did the trade deficit the Canadians had feared become a reality. New France had built a fort at Creve Couer on the Illinois River and lost it when it became involved in a tribal war between the Iroquois and Illinois Indians. In 1682 they built a fort at Starved Rock known as Saint Louis. It survived, but as it was located below the confluence of the Illinois and Mississippi Rivers, France claimed it. France had divided the territory so that everything north of the confluence of the rivers belonged to New France and everything south and west to France. The boundary line extended northwest along the Mississippi and eastward from the Illinois into the Ohio watershed and along the Appalachians to the St. Lawrence. France had the plum. The English, through constant immigration, were moving west of the Appalachians.

The French were unique in their approach to dealing with the tribes. They looked upon the Indians as simple children, referred to them as such and moved in with them; adopting dress, language, paint and often hairstyle of a particular tribe. They were not against marriage into the tribe. They would act as counsel and settle tribal disputes and in at least two instances brought about alliances. They traded fairly with the tribes, and would go on tribal hunts and raiding parties, although they, for the most part, held back from any of the fighting using the logic that the alleged enemy might well become a trading source in the future. They were extremely diplomatic with the tribes, realizing that an individual or tribe could turn hostile over the slightest social wrong.

The English approach to the tribes was the exact opposite. Indians had a place and they should keep it. The religious zealots attempted conversion at every occasion, regardless of the aftermath. Their approach was simple. All the Indian believed in was wrong and only their way was right. The French Catholic priests in Canada were far more successful, as they blended the two religions together, being ever tolerant of the Indians' habits and customs. The majority of the colonists felt the tribes were a nuisance, there to be cheated, robbed, dispossessed, killed, enslaved and used as they saw fit.

The blatant arrogance on the part of the English toward the Indians would slowly drag them into the vortex of the war. For out of this arrogance came the Pequot War over the alleged act of theft. (Some Pequots attacked a fishing boat, killed the crew and stole the supplies.) Then the Narragansett War, or King Phillip's War, over the slaying of a Christian Indian by a non-Christian Indian and finally the outright cheating of the Delawares out of their land in 1737 served as catalysts to place the British in the center of the war.

Thomas Penn, William Penn's son, cheated the Delaware out of 1,200 square miles of land. The land was to stretch from present-day Wrightstown, Pennsylvania, to a point as far into the woods as a man could walk in one and one-half days. To the Indian this was roughly 25 miles per day with stops. The settlers, in preparation, cut a path through the woods and ended up walking some 60 miles. The so-called "Walking Purchase" contained all the Delaware land.

The net result was the total annihilation of the Pequots, Narragansetts and several allied nations as nations. The survivors joined the "Huron" in Canada.

The Delawares left Pennsylvania to settle in Canada, with the majority of them remaining neutral. This was a far cry from the days of Plymouth Colony when the English colonists depended on the Indians for survival.

Not only were the English turning their Indian allies into enemies, the French and Hurons were raiding into northern New York with unnerving regularity.

Saratoga Springs, or the Schuyler Patent which Peter Schuyler had purchased from the Mohawks in 1684, was receiving much of their attention. Saratoga Springs was the site of tribal hunting grounds and the junction of two main trails; one from Canada and another from the west through the Mohawk Valley. The British had built a fort here known as Fort Clinton and in 1747 a mixed force of 700 French and Indians attacked the fort, taking 45 prisoners and 28 scalps. The Schuyler home was burned and the fort abandoned. Albany was left as the northernmost fortified British settlement. The French had raided Saratoga two years earlier in a hit-and-run attack which carried over to the settlement of Hoosick. That raid netted them 100 prisoners plus an unknown number of scalps. Scalping raids were almost a weekly and sometimes a daily event, with outlying homesteads being laid to waste.

By 1754 the situation in the New World was tense. France was in Canada and Louisiana. It needed the Ohio watershed as the most direct connecting corridor. To assure this, they had established a fort in western Pennsylvania at what is now Pittsburgh, known as Fort Duquesne. They had also established Forts Niagara and Frontenac on Lake

Ontario for the same reason. The English were moving inland from the coast and something had to give.

The rupture occurred when Washington ambushed a French patrol, disobeying orders to avoid all contact with the French. Later in the year he would be defeated soundly by the French at a small fort call Necessity. The frontier passed through another bloody winter and finally in the spring of 1755 the British sent one of their finest officers with two regiments to the colonies.

Chapter Three

A HUMILIATION OF ARMS

General Edward Braddock was considered one of the finest officers of his time. He was excellent as an administrator and exceptional as a field commander. His one shortcoming was that he was trained on the fields of Europe, not in the wilderness of the New World. In the summer of 1755 he was in that wilderness advancing on the French at Fort Duquesne. This was the first of four phases of battle plan he had drawn which, if it succeeded, would keep the French from the Ohio watershed.

Braddock had a command composed of 1,400 regulars, 450 militia, 262 independents, 300 axmen, 38 sailors (to handle the artillery train) and 54 women, one of them his mistress. The command moved slowly and as it neared Duquesne, Braddock began to fear that the French would flee. This fear was based on information given him by a Delaware Indian who had come into camp after being at Fort Duquesne. According to the Indian, there were only some 50 men at the fort, but they were expecting 400 more shortly; however, they proposed to blow up the fort if the British appeared. After conferring with his officers, including Washington who was with him, he decided to split his command, sending a flying column ahead to engage the French. The flying column was composed of some 1,200 men of the 2,100 odd who made up the command. Included in this number were 33 seamen.

Braddock and Washington were both with the flying column. They did engage the French, but it was on French terms. Lieutenant Charles Spendelow, R.N., of H.M.S. *Gibraltar*, who was in charge of the naval detachment assigned to Braddock kept a journal which is excerpted here. It is taken somewhat out of chronological order to bring the battle into perspective.

On 8 July 1755 Braddock and the flying column were camped within eight miles of Fort Duquesne. It was by unanimous agreement of all the officers that they should pass the Monongahela River in the morning and the advance party should march at 2:00 A.M. to secure the passage.

On 9 July the advance party of 400 men marched about 7:00 A.M. Some Indians rushed out of the bushes, but did no harm. The party went on and secured both passes of the river and at 11:00 A.M. the main body began to cross with colors flying, drums beating and fifes playing the Grenadier's March and soon formed when they thought that the French would not attack them, as they might have done it with such advantage in crossing the Monongahela. The advance party was one-quarter mile in front of the main body the rear of which was just over the river, when the front was attacked. Two grenadier companies formed the flank, the Piquots with the rest of the men, were covering the carpenters while they were cutting the roads.

Mr. Engineer Gordon was the first man to see the enemy, being in front of the carpenters, marking and picketing the road for them. He stated that when he first discovered the enemy, they were on the run, which plainly showed they were just come from Fort Duquesne, and their principle intent was to secure the river passage. Upon sighting each other, the French officer who was dressed like an Indian with a gorget, waved his hat by way of signal to disperse the enemy to right and left, forming a half moon.

The first fire the enemy gave was in front, and they likewise gualed [sic] the Piquets in flank, so that in a few minutes, the grenadiers were nearly cut to pieces and in great confusion as were the company of carpenters. As soon as the main body heard that the front was attacked, they instantly advanced to secure them but found them retreating, upon which the general ordered the artillery to draw up and the battalion to form. By this time the enemy had attacked the main body which faced to the right and left and engaged them, but could not see whom they fired at.

The main body was drawn up in an open road and the trees were "excessive thick round them." The French had possession of the hill to the right which, consequently, gave them an excellent advantage. Many British officers would later comment that they never saw more than five of the enemy at one time during the whole action.

According to the lieutenant, the soldiers were encouraged to make many attempts by the officers (who behaved gloriously) to take the hill, but they had been so intimidated before by seeing their comrades scalped in their sight and such numbers falling that as they advanced up towards the hill and saw their officers being picked off, which was generally the case, they turned to the right about and retired down the hill.

When the general perceived and was concerned that the soldiers would not fight in a regular manner without officers, he divided them into small parties and endeavored to surround the enemy, but by this time, the major part of the officers were either killed or wounded and, in short, the soldiers were totally deaf to the commands and persuasions of the few officers who were left unhurt.

The general had four horses shot under him before he was wounded toward the latter part of the action when he was put into a wagon with great difficulty as he was very solicitous for being left in the field. The retreat now became general, and it was the opinion of many people that had we greater numbers, it would have been just the same thing as our advance party never regaining the ground they were first attacked upon. It was extremely lucky they pursued no farther than the first crossing of the river, but they killed and scalped everyone they met with.

The general died on 12 July. Returns show that 896 enlisted were killed or wounded. Of 86 officers, 63 were killed or wounded. The naval detachment had one midshipman, one boatswain's mate and seven able-bodied seamen killed and two able-bodied's wounded. Of the 54 women, only four returned; seven were taken prisoner. Of the 43 unaccounted for, we know eight were found totally stripped, scalped and mutilated. According to an unidentified source, Braddock's mistress was also killed. She was captured by a group of French cadets. A group of some 20 odd Indians appeared and demanded the woman. The cadets became frightened for their own lives and let the Indians have her. The Indians ripped her clothes off and raped her repeatedly. They then tied her to a tree and used her as a target for arrows; the Indians aimed carefully so that her life ebbed away as slowly as possible. When she was dead she was cut into pieces, boiled and eaten.

Materiel loss as a result of this action was four 6-pounders, two 12-pounders, three howitzers, eight cohorns, 51 carriages of provisions, ammunition, hospital stores, the general's private chest which had about $1,000 and 200 horses loaded with officer's baggage.

Braddock's defeat was a decided setback and, to complicate the issue, the French captured all his papers, including his four-phase plan. The other phases were to use Fort Oswego as a base of operations to go down the St. Lawrence River, an attack up Lake Champlain (the other Little Lake) to Montreal, and lastly, the removal of the Acadians from Nova Scotia.

The French force that defeated Braddock was approximately 900 men in strength. Roughly two-thirds of it was Indian. The balance was predominantly *coureurs de bois* (fur traders and woodsmen), with a few regulars. The force was under the command of Captain Daniel-Hyacinthe-Marie Lienard de Beaujeu, a Canadian militia officer. His number two was Captain Jean-Daniel Dumas.

Captain Beaujeu was one of the few and one of the first of the French party to be killed. It was he who waved his hat to his party as a signal. He was, according to Spendelow's journal, dressed Indian fashion with only his officer's gorget marking him as an officer. The French loss was 28 killed and wounded.

Some of the British force present at Braddock's defeat would again fight the French and Indians. Some eventually would fight against each other. Those who became well-known historical figures included Sir John St. Clair, Lt. Col. R. Burton, Lt. Col. Thomas Gage, Capt. Horatio Gates, and Ens. Harry Gordon (Engr), as well as Lt. Col. George Washington and a militiaman by the name of Daniel Boone.

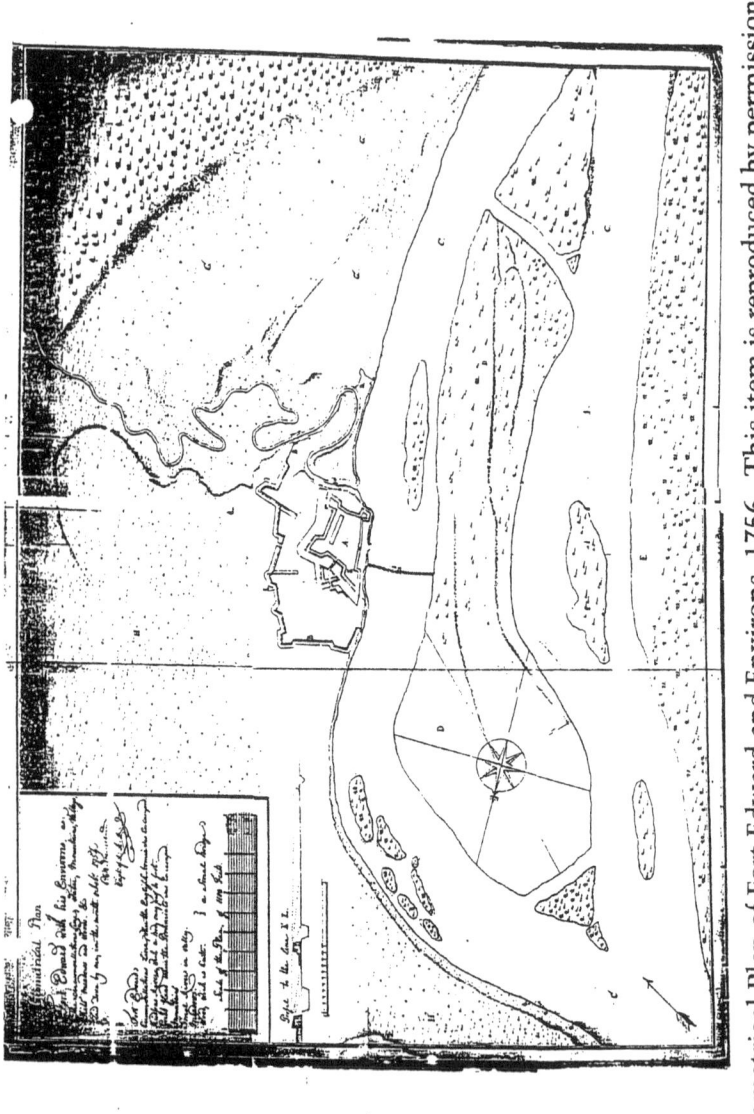

Geometrical Plan of Fort Edward and Environs, 1756. This item is reproduced by permission of The Huntington Library, San Marino, California. Kashnor Collection, HM15443.

Chapter Four

BEGINNING OF THE END

With Braddock's plans in hand, Governor Vaudreuil of Canada was able to stop the British at Oswego, which was his main concern as it was the most direct line to the Ohio watershed. In the meantime, Sir William Johnson was to build a fort at "The Great Carrying Place" on the Hudson River, approximately 17 miles south of Lake George.

This fort was to serve as a point to retire to should the attack up Lake Champlain fail. It was Fort Edward, known as Lydius to the French. The construction of the fort was charged to Col. Phineas Lyman, and its design was charged to Capt. William Eyre of the 44th Regiment of Foot.

When Johnson arrived at the Fort Edward construction site, he learned of a buildup of French troops at Fort St. Frederic on the upper end of Lake Champlain. This buildup was superior to his command in numbers. It was obvious that a surprise attack, or any attack, was out of the question. Orders were given to build another fort at the south end of Lake George to stem any advance by the French and to serve as a base of operations against the French. In late August 1755, Johnson moved the greater part of his troops to Lake George and set up camp at what would be Fort William Henry. The command was given to Brevet General Lyman. Second-in-command was Colonel Williams. Johnson was district or area commander.

The French, in a defensive move, after reading Braddock's plan, had sent a force from Montreal to Fort Frederic, or Saint Frederic as they called it, under General Baron von Dieskau. They arrived at the fort on 1 September 1755. The force was composed of 600 militia, 200 regulars and 700 Hurons.

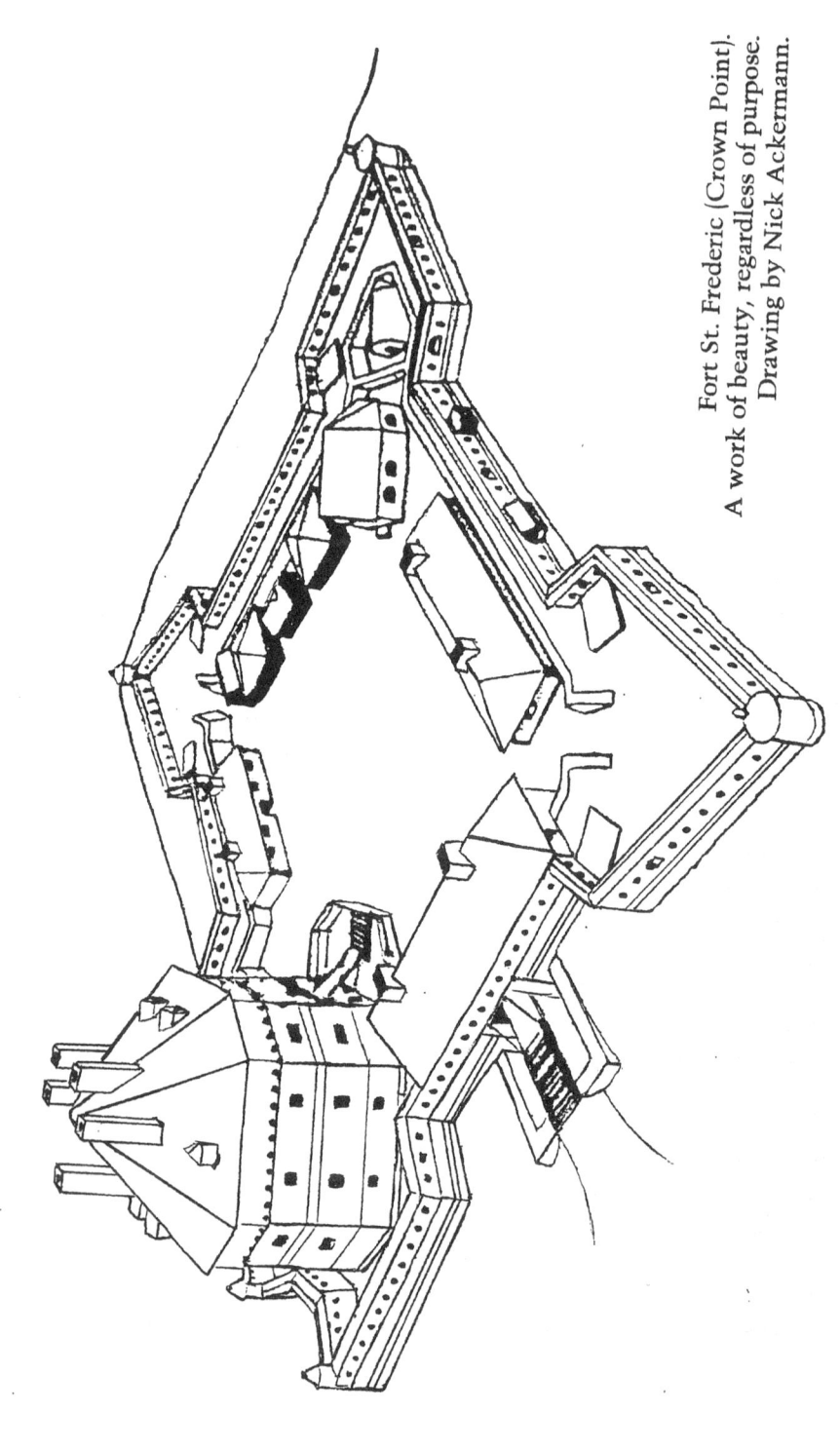

Fort St. Frederic (Crown Point). A work of beauty, regardless of purpose. Drawing by Nick Ackermann.

Ironically, Fort William Henry was built for the same purpose that the French built Fort St. Frederic, or Crown Point as it was known to the British. Fort St. Frederic had been built in 1731 and was used as a base of operations throughout King George's War. It was from here that the force that destroyed Fort Clinton at the Schuyler Plantation or Patent departed and a year later a larger force departed to sack Saratoga, Schenectady and Albany.

Simultaneously, the British determined that Fort William Henry was needed while the French reinforced Fort St. Frederic. The French also decided to build Fort Carillon or Ticonderoga. They started construction on the fort in 1755 and finally completed it in 1757.

In September 1755, Dieskau learned from a British prisoner at Fort St. Frederic that Fort Edward had only 500 troops and was just half completed. He was aware of the construction at Lake George, but felt that if he could destroy Fort Edward, he would effectively cut off the troops at Lake George and set back the British plans again. He ordered the troops on a forced march carrying only a blanket, bear skin, extra shirt, one extra pair of shoes and their weapons. Using a secondary line of travel down Wood Creek east of the lake, he was two miles from Fort Edward by sunset of 7 September 1755.

When the Hurons in Dieskau's command learned the fort was defended by cannon they refused to attack. This added fuel to his dislike of the Indians. As he already noted, "They drive us crazy from morning till night. There is no end to their demands. They have already eaten five oxen and as many hogs, without counting the kegs of brandy they have drunk." Montcalm would suffer the same problems.

Dieskau decided instead to attack Lake George, and then return to Fort Edward. In his attack orders he told his Hurons not to take time to scalp the wounded or dead until the British either had been defeated or had surrendered, as they could kill ten men in the time it took to scalp one. Dieskau moved north toward the lake at daybreak on 8 September 1755, using the military road the British had built. Johnson had approximately 2,700 men at the lake.

A Plan of the Town and Fort of Carillon at Ticonderoga,

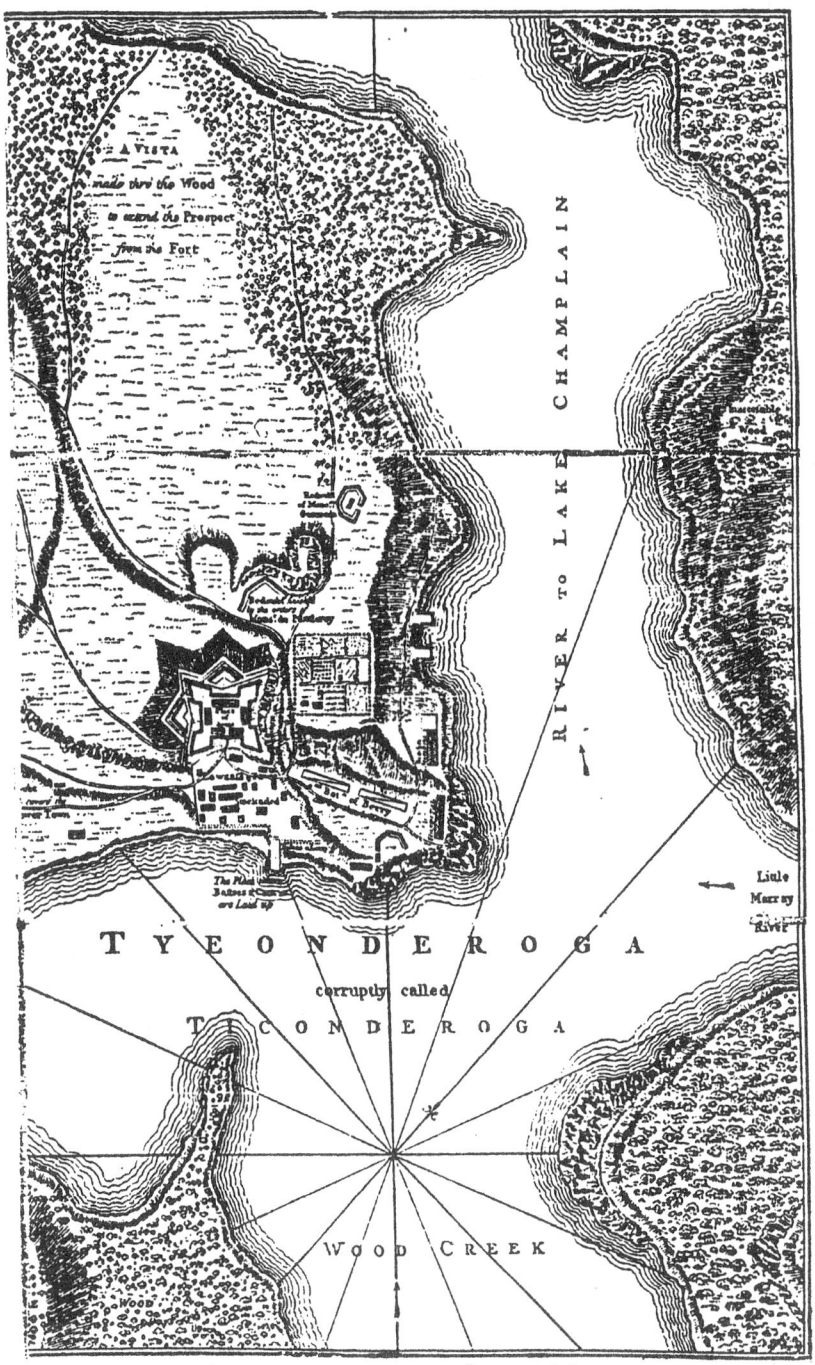

July 1758. *Fort Ticonderoga Museum.*

They had more cannon than Fort Edward and were reasonably well entrenched with fortified breastworks. He was aware of the French in the area and had sent a messenger to Fort Edward to alert them. The messenger never got there. Johnson, with good reason, felt he was in a bad position. He knew Fort Edward must have relief. If the French got control, he would be cut off from Albany and retreat would be impossible.

After a conference with the officers, Johnson dispatched 1,000 troops under Colonel Ephraim Williams to Fort Edward on the morning of 8 September 1755. Lt. Col. Nathaniel Whiting was Williams' second-in-command and, along with the troops, was a group of Mohawk Indians under their chief, King Hendrick.

The French were alerted to the British and set up an ambush similar to the one that had defeated Braddock. The British were taken by surprise. Williams' horse was shot from under him and as he scrambled to the top of a rock he was killed instantly. King Hendrick was pinned to the ground by his dead horse and killed by a French bayonet. Colonel Whiting set up a rear guard action and passed the survivors through this and back to Lake George.

The battle at the lake lasted for some six hours before the French broke off and left to recover their baggage where they had left it by a pond to one side of the military road.

The intensity of the battle was described by Surgeon Williams, "It was the most awful my eyes ever beheld. There seemed to be nothing but thunder and lightning and perpetual pillars of smoke." Another unidentified soldier wrote, "The hailstones from Heaven were never much thicker than their bullets came." Dieskau was heard to remark of the British, "They fight like devils."

The acting commander of Fort Edward, Colonel Joseph Blanchard of the New Hampshire militia, had also learned of the presence of the French and sent a detachment of 200 to 250 men under Captains McGinnis and Folsom of the New Hampshire militia to join Johnson at Fort William Henry. The French baggage park was discovered and an ambush was set up. There were New York militia in this party as well and one story says Robert Rogers and some of his Rangers were with the party, but there is no evidence to support this.

It was evening when the French arrived at their makeshift baggage park. They were exhausted and hungry. The colonials waited for them to start their meal and then attacked. A heavy engagement followed during which both Captains McGinnis and Folsom were killed. The French were routed. So many of them were killed that when their bodies were rolled into the pond they literally formed a bridge across the water. To this day, the pond is still referred to as Bloody Pond and is marked as a historic site.

This was the first major engagement that the British had won. The upper hand was gained for a period of time, but the British never followed through and the French soon were in the fore again. Baron von Dieskau was 54 years old at the time of the battle. He was wounded four times, taken prisoner by the British and literally saved from the Mohawk allies of the British by William Johnson when Johnson had him placed in his personal tent. Dieskau remained a prisoner until 1763, and he died four years later of complications from the wounds he received at the Battle of Lake George.

Colonel Ephraim Williams, killed during the ambush, was 40 years of age. He was from Massachusetts and had seen service as a captain during King George's War. His will directed that the property he owned in Williamstown, Massachusetts be used as a free school. It was from this school that Williams College developed.

Although William Johnson is generally given credit for winning the Battle of Lake George, he had little, if anything, to do with it. Early on in the engagement he was slightly wounded and General Lyman took over the command.

Johnson came to the colonies as a young man from Ireland to manage a vast tract of land that his uncle had purchased from the Mohawks. He soon became a great favorite of the Mohawks and they adopted him into the tribe. Eventually, he became a sachem of the tribe and

Bloody Pond. An unknown number of French and Indians call it their last resting place.

married Molly Brant, sister of Joseph Brant, the British-university-educated war chief of the Mohawks.

Johnson on his own took all the credit for the battle at Lake George. He never mentioned General Lyman in any of the dispatches or reports. He went so far as to rename Fort Lyman, Fort Edward, gaining a bow from the crown in so doing. He went abroad and was celebrated as a hero. The king made him a present of a baronetcy and Parliament gave him a gift of 5,000 pounds.

King Hendrick, chief of the Mohawks, was born Tiyanoga in 1680. He became a Christian and ally of the British. He represented the Mohawks at the Albany Congress of 1754 where he proved to be one of the mainstays in a treaty between the seven British colonies and the Iroquois confederation. All the confederation signed the treaty except the Delawares who were not members of the confederation and were still smarting from the land deal of 1737.

Hendrick was opposed to the force Johnson wanted to send out from Lake George stating, "If they are to fight, they are too few; if they are to be killed, they are too many." His statement proved to be correct – 200 were killed, including Hendrick, in what history has termed "The Bloody Morning Scout."

By late 1756, British fortunes were at an all-time low. They had no outposts left in the west, the last fort falling in August 1756. Fort Oswego was located on the west side of the Oswego River at its terminus with Lake Ontario. It was, in fact, three forts in one.

Fort Oswego had been built in 1727. Located on a high promontory, it was built of stone. It was two stories tall and was surrounded by a stone wall. At a later date a wooden stockade was built on the eastern side of the river and called Fort Ontario. A third fort was under construction in 1756 to be called Fort George.

The purpose of the fort was to protect the Mohawk Valley. The fort commander was Colonel James Mercer, apparently of the Massachusetts militia. Due to its somewhat isolated location the fort was always poorly supplied, although it maintained a garrison strength of some 1,700 to 2,000 men.

The French and Indians constantly harassed the British forts after the onset of the war and by May 1756 the forts were under siege. Montcalm led the French, who soon were so close to the walls of Fort Ontario that the British forces evacuated it in the night and withdrew to Fort Oswego. What few troops were at Fort George were recalled to Fort Oswego and the siege of that fort began in earnest on 10 August 1756.

The French, taking advantage of the location of Fort Ontario, placed Fort Oswego under artillery fire from a range of some 500 yards with devastating results. Colonel Mercer was killed by a direct hit from an artillery shot. Within hours the remainder of the garrison sued for surrender and finally had to accept Montcalm's unconditional surrender terms. The Indians killed and scalped all the sick, wounded and stragglers. Two more prisoners were killed on the way to Montreal. The fort fell on 14 August 1756, with the French leaving on 21 August 1756 as both forts burned to smoking piles of rubble.

Some of the cannon used by the French had been captured from Braddock and a year would serve at Fort William Henry.

Beginning of the End / 29

Photograph of the reconstructed Fort William Henry.
Courtesy of Richard K. Dean.

Chapter Five

PRELIMINARIES

Construction of Fort William Henry was completed in November 1756 and command of it given to now-Major Eyre of the 44th Foot. It was a ramparted enclosure with four bastions, incorporated into the ramparts which were cross-log, earth-filled, with the magazine under the northeast bastion and shops for maintenance and storage of equipment. It measured some 150 feet across and some 250 feet in length, excluding bastions, which extended the width another 50 feet and the length another 100 feet. Excluding ramparts and bastions, it contained approximately 13,500 square feet. The hospital command building was on the north wall, barracks for enlisted men on the east and west walls and officers' quarters on the south wall. There was a guard room under the west barracks.

The fort was parapeted, with glacis and moat. To the south and west the moat was equipped with chevaux-de-frise. The lake was to the north and a marsh to the east.

The fort could accommodate 36 cannon, but was equipped with 17 of various sizes. The cannon were predominantly 9- and 12-pounders. There were at least two 6-pounders and several mortars. The cannon were mounted on both garrison and field carriages. The garrison carriages allowed the gun to be moved back from the firing port to be reloaded.

Camp William Henry extended some 400 yards to the west, roughly 65 yards to the south and approximately 100 feet to the marsh on the east. This area was more than adequately covered by the cannon whose range at level was 700 to 1,300 feet. With a 45° angle, the range increased to 10,744 from 15,657 feet. There is some evidence that there was at least one 20-pounder, possibly two. Their range on the level was 1,800 feet and with a 45° angle, 17,850 feet.

Mortars were 2-1/4 or 3-1/2 inch and used primarily for throwing grenades. The military musket "Brown Bess" which had a maximum range of 1,000 feet, was penetrating at 500 feet and most effective at 300 feet or less.

The fort was built, as was Fort Edward, to house 400 men and officers. It had several points of vulnerability, such as a large garden area to the northwest along the shore within camp limits and beyond that approximately a mile away what was known as Artillery Cove. There was a second garden to the south and, until destroyed during a French attack in March 1757, an area known as Lower Town, just to the immediate east of the fort along the shore. This area included some storage buildings and a ship-building yard. There was only one gate wide enough to allow a wagon through and no sally ports. In 1756 a British army engineer advised after inspecting the nearly completed fort that it was weak on its west side, the walls should be raised about three feet, as they were only 17 feet high, and a wedge-shaped outer works, known as a ravelin, should be added to the west wall. This was never done. Later the weakest point was the military road to the south which could be cut by a skirmish line, leaving the fort totally isolated.

The British had a small navy at Fort William Henry. By the end of 1756, it consisted of two sloops of 20 tons each, mounted with four swivels each and two sloops of 30 tons mounted with unknown armament, although it was suggested that they were armed with four Royals each. These were small cannon, larger than swivels, but not carrying a pound designation that this author has been able to locate. They also had three large scows, a large number of whaleboats and a great many bateaux.

There were two companies of Rangers under the command of Captains Hobbs and Speakman at Fort William Henry. They had their own entrenched camp. Captain Hobbs, known as "The Fighting Deacon," died of smallpox and was replaced by Captain John Stark. Captain Speakman would eventually be wounded by the French, captured by the Huron and literally butchered to death.

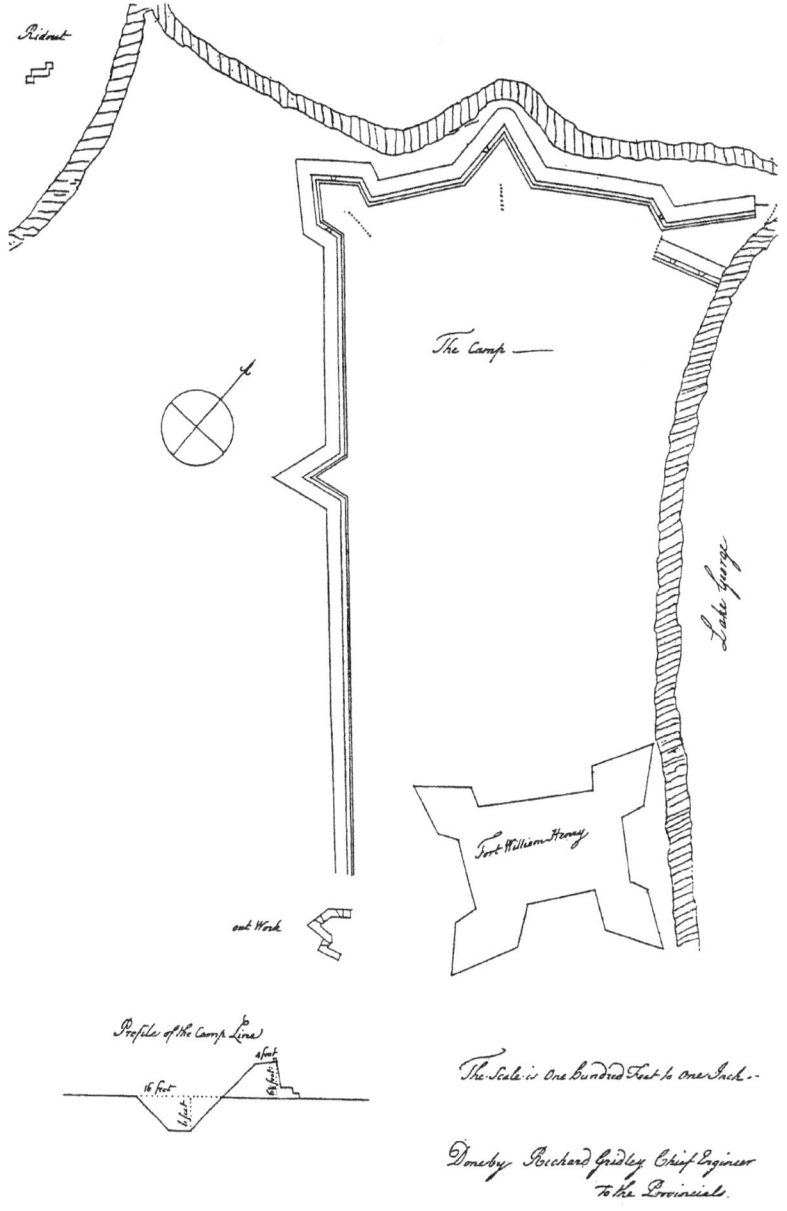

Plan of Fort William Henry, 1756. This item is reproduced by permission of *The Huntington Library, San Marino, California.* Kashnor Collection, HM15406.

Fort William Henry: Corner of fort headquarters, showing entrance to fort magazine, fort well and small mortar. Steps and ramp lead to rampart and bastion.

Headquarters and hospital building at Fort William Henry.

It was during this time that a 15-year-old boy from Connecticut who had lied about his age and having his mother's approval showed up at Fort William Henry with the Connecticut militia. It wasn't long before a guardian showed up and took him home. Benedict Arnold was determined to be a soldier.

The winter of 1755-56 brought a temporary end to military operations other than hit-and-run raids by the Rangers or their French counterparts. Washington wrote of that time, "Every day we have accounts of cruelty and barbarity as are shocking to human nature. It is not possible to conceive the situation and danger of this miserable country. Such numbers of French and Indians are all around that no road is safe." Another chronicler of that era wrote, "It was a common sight for the husband to see the wife of his bosom, her head cut off and the children's blood drunk like water by these bloody and cruel savages."

The Niagara Frontier

On 18 May 1756, England declared war on France. In the New World the war had contracted from the western frontier of Pennsylvania, Maryland and Virginia to an elongated corridor extending from the Atlantic seaboard of Canada down the St. Lawrence River to Montreal and south along Lake Champlain and Lake George into the Mohawk and Hudson River valleys. The British had a defensive line running from the northwest to the southeast. For some unknown reason they never reopened Fort Anne, which was located northeast of Fort William Henry and had been in use during King George's War; nor did they rebuild Fort Clinton at Saratoga. This would have given them a strong line of defense, cutting all available routes south. As it was, the French and Hurons infiltrated with impunity, using Wood Creek between Fort William Henry and the ruins of Fort Anne.

The area was referred to as the Niagara Frontier. The raids were sudden and brutal. The British regulars were always a day late and the frontier was under constant siege. When the British were not giving chase, they were busy strengthening both Fort William Henry and Fort Edward to the point that by 1 November 1756, Governor Vaudreuil felt that it would be difficult to besiege Fort William Henry and impossible to besiege Fort Edward. He also felt that the British would use Fort William Henry to stage a thrust against Forts Carillon and St. Frederic, the outermost defenses of Montreal.

Pierre de Rigaud de Vaudreuil de Cavagnial, Marquis de Vaudreuil was the son of a former governor general of New France. He was born in Quebec on 22 November 1698. He was commissioned an ensign in the colonial regulars in 1708 and promoted to lieutenant in 1711. He was presented to the French court at the age of 13. He learned the administration of the colony from his father, who died in 1725. In 1733 he became the governor of Trois-Rivieres. He became the governor general of Louisiana in 1743 and served in that capacity until 1755. It was while serving in this capacity that he learned the much feared trade deficit would be a while in coming as the Canadians were much better organized and the arrival of ships much more a sure thing. By the time he became governor general of New France in 1755 he was a skilled administrator, wise to the corruption within the system and a capable leader of troops. He would eventually order the Marquis de Lévis to surrender Montreal to spare his people in any further death and destruction. As the French government was looking for someone to blame for the loss of the war, he would be put in the Bastille in March of 1762, released in May 1762 and finally totally exonerated in December 1763. He died in quiet retirement in his Paris home on 4 August 1778.

By late 1756, the Marquis de Montcalm was in Canada by order of the king of France. He was to take over the military, although the governor general had final authority. Vaudreuil, exercising his authority, devised a plan that would, if successful, act as a setback of enormous size to the British. He felt that a winter attack on Fort William Henry would serve this purpose. To this end he dispatched his brother Rigaud with 1,500 men from Fort Saint Jean, just south of Montreal, during the third week of February

1757. The plan was to attack Fort William Henry on St. Patrick's Day, reasoning that the Irish regiment at the fort would be celebrating and off guard.

Chapter Six

THE FIRST GO ROUND

As Vaudreuil had guessed, the 48th were enjoying St. Patrick's Day to their fullest capacity. However, Vaudreuil had a nemesis who would destroy his surprise attack.

During the winter of 1756-1757, there were two Ranger companies stationed at Fort William Henry; one under the command of Captain Humphrey "The Fighting Deacon" Hobbs, and the other under the command of Captain Thomas Spikeman. (It is of note that Captain Spikeman is also referred to as Sparkman or Speakman. According to Major Robert Rogers, his name was Spikeman.) When Capt. Hobbs died of smallpox in February 1757, Rogers promoted Lt. John Stark to captain and sent him to Fort William Henry to take over Hobbs' company.

Captain John Stark was always the cool, cautious gentleman soldier although a somewhat severe man, admired by his men as a fighter and woodsman *par excellence*. He was born in Londonderry, New Hampshire in 1728. He served in King George's War and for the duration of the French and Indian War served with the Rangers. On one occasion he was captured by the Huron. They decided that he should run the gauntlet, which few people survived. He approached the two lines of Indians at a walk and as the first Indian brave moved toward him, he quickly grabbed the Indian and threw him across his shoulders. He then proceeded to run the gauntlet with the Indian across his shoulders absorbing the blows meant for him.

Captain Stark, for reasons known only to himself, suspected the French would attempt an assault around St. Patrick's Day. The Rangers, having no extra grog supply, approached the captain and requested an extra issue. The captain refused on the grounds that his sprained wrist (he did have one) kept him from signing the commissary order for the extra grog. To cut off illegal consumption of grog, he also shut down Sutler Levi on the 15th of March. The captain then sent three patrols up Lake George. Within 24 hours, all had reported in with the information that there were three French columns approaching, one column on each side of the lake and one down the center.

There is a story that the French were discovered when the British saw their camp fires. The French traveled 180 miles on a cold march. They used no camp fires, lived on cold rations, slept in bearskins, used dog sledges to haul their provisions and snow shoes and skates to make the march. Rigaud Vaudreuil was an adept woodsman and soldier. He would not sacrifice his mission for the sake of a warming fire.

Rigaud de Vaudreuil was born Francois-Pierre de Rigaud de Vaudreuil on 8 February 1708 in Montreal. He was the son of a governor general and brother to another. At least one historical writer has referred to him as the nephew of the governor general and another called him the illegitimate half-breed brother of the governor general. He held commissions in both the navy and army. He was a soldier, fur trader and land owner. He had been active as a soldier during King George's War and taken prisoner in 1755 when the ship he was returning to Canada on was captured by the British. Imprisoned in England, he escaped to France, returning to Canada in 1756. At the time of the attack on Fort William Henry he was the governor of Trois-Rivières.

The French knew the element of surprise was lost when they found the snowshoe trails of the Rangers. They halted at Diamond Island, which is a short distance up the lake from the fort, on the 17th. On the 18th they started a sniper fire attack on the fort.

Captain Stark had notified Major Eyre, the fort commander, of the intelligence his Rangers had obtained and the major set his fort to receive an attack.

The following letter from Major Eyre to Lord Loudon, dated 26 March 1757, sets out the details of the battle.

Fort William Henry
26 March 1757
My Lord,
   Last Saturday, being the 19th instant, about one o'clock in the morning, a noise of axes was heard, that seem'd to be about three miles from the Fort; and a small light was seen upon the East Side, and a very considerable way down the Lake. This gave the alarm. Two hours or more after this, the enemy's approaches were heard very distinctly upon the ice, with their whole army. This, we afterwards learn'd and also that they had 300 scaling ladders, and all the apparatus necessary for a general assault. This drew upon them a smart fire of artillery and small arms which obliged the main body to retire. After this they attempted to set on fire one of the sloops and the batteaus but were prevented. Other efforts were used before daylight to accomplish this affair, which they likewise failed in. At the break of day the enemy withdrew and a few men were sent out to see what they could discover, who found a few scaling ladders and several other emplements, to set the vessels and boats on fire.
   By prisoners we afterwards took, we found the enemy were very numerous; one of their accounts is they were 1650, another upwards of two thousand, consisting of Regulars, Colony Troops (or their Independent Company's) Canadians and Indians.
   The enemy soon after they disappeared began to show themselves again on the lake, and on each side of it and, by degrees, their appearance grew more formidable. They were filing off in large bodies to surround us and at the same time kept a heavy fire of small arms upon the garrison. The fire of our artillery checked their approach and by what we could discover made their different detachments retire, for they made no attempt that they only fired smartly, with muskuetry. The next morning being the 20th, another attempt was made by their whole army, to storm the

place, but by the heavy fire from the garrison, were drove back. This happened very early. Not succeeding they set on fire, two sloops, and burnt almost all our batteaus, and when daylight appeared drew off. About mid-day and their army were seen marching across the lake in regular bodys and seemed very numerous, as if returning towards Ticonderoga; but presently after a few men were seen coming towards the Fort (with a red flag) on the ice, who made signals at half a miles distance to have some one sent to speak to them. I complied with this and sent an Officer and four men, with another flag to meet them. Presently, after one of our own people brought me a letter which was from Mons. De Vaudreuil, Commander of the French Army, a copy of which I enclose, in consequence of the letter I sent an Officer to bring in Mons. Francois le Mercier blindfolded. The substance of whose message I have likewise enclosed.

    I desired him to make my compliments to the General, and tell him, my fixt resolution was to defend His Majesty's Garrison to the last extremity. Upon this he was carried back blindfolded as he came and soon after their army were seen to move toward us, every thing in readiness for a general assault; and tho we were sickly, a general firmness could be discovered by the behavior of the troops, so as to give great hopes, they do their part. The Officers behaved with the greatest diligence, care and resolution. The enemys fire was soon renewed, by some detached partys; the main body kept at a distance. That night or early the next morning, a third general assault was undertaken, which they likewise failed in. They not succeeding set on fire two storehouses, (one of them a good deal of provisions) on one side; a provincial storehouse, and all the Rangers hutts (within side their picketted fort) on the other. These different fires burnt with such violence, so as to make one apprehend, at one side of the fort, that the other or opposite quarters were in flames. Yet happily by proper care and vigilance within

side, no damage was done. In this situation we
continued the most part of the night, a perfect silence
was observed and a constant fire kept upon the enemy
when ever we could make any discovery by means of
the fires, or before were made by list'ning with the
utmost attention. The different times that the enemy
intended a general assault under the cover of darkness,
they were wholly baffled, by steadily keeping up to
this last method, for our eyes at these times, were of
no use to us, being so excessively dark. The next day
being Monday the 21st, the enemy withdrew at
daybreak, in their usual way. This morning very few of
their straglers remain'd and about nine or 10 o'clock it
began to snow and continued so the whole day and
night, during which time the fire on both sides in a
great measure ceased, and we could not discover they
attempt anything during that time. Tuesday the 22d
early in the morning, the enemy seem'd resolved to
burn the sloop up on the stocks; several times they
were beat off, but still persevered and by means of
combustibles and dry faggots, which they brought
from their encampment at last effected their design;
during the whole time they frequently attempted to set
fire to our picketted storehouse, that is next to the
lake, but were always bravely beat off. The last efforts
must have been used to preserve this place as it could
not fail of setting the garrison in flames if they had
succeeded. The sloop upon the stocks continued
blazing till broad day on Wednesday, when we
discovered a man in the swamp seemingly wounded; a
small party was ordered to bring him in; at which
time, another of the enemy was found behind a pile of
chord wood; which last I apprehend was afraid of going
off after the sloop was in a blaze, as no body could
move there abouts, but must have been discovered.
These are the prisoners we now have; a third was
brought in, who had scarcely life when taken into the
hospital. A little time after this the enemy wholly
disappeared.

> The whaleboats, scows or gundolas & bayboats escaped the conflagration. – We have had seven men slightly wounded. The prisoners tell us our artillery had a good effect.
> I am
> > My Lord
> > > with great respect
> > > > Your Lordship's
> > > > > Most Obedient
> > > > > > Humble Servant
> > > > > > > Will: Eyre
> > > > > > > Maj. To 44th Regiment
>
> P.S. – I send the Intelligence and Declaration of the two prisoners, and likewise a list of the things they inform me their Army were provid'd with for this expedition.
>
> Strength of the Garrison of Fort Wm. Henry when the enemy came before it.
>
> | | |
> |---|---|
> | Regulars fit for duty | 274 |
> | Rangers ditto | <u>72</u> |
> | Total Well | 346 |
> | Sick Regulars and Rangers | <u>128</u> |
> | Total Sick and Well | 474 |
> | Rt. Honble, the Earl of Loudon | |

On the return trip to Canada the French sustained additional casualties to frostbite, exposure and snow blindness.

Rigaud de Vaudreuil would later become the governor of Montreal. With the end of the war he returned to France, although a Canadian by birth, and died there on 24 August 1779.

After the war Capt. John Stark became a farmer again until the American Revolution. He fought at Bunker Hill, saw service at Princeton and Trenton and fought in the

Quebec campaign. He defeated a British column at Bennington which resulted in Gentleman Johnny Burgoyne's surrender at Saratoga. He retired a brigadier general of the U.S. Army.

Mons. Francois le Mercier, the French officer who carried the messages between Eyre and Vaudreuil, would at a later date again be at Fort William Henry.

Major William Eyre would leave Fort William Henry in mid-April 1757. He served three more years with the 44th and left the colonies for England. As he returned to his home in Ireland, the ship he was on floundered off the coast of Ireland and went down with all hands.

The March attack had its desired effect. It served to unnerve the British and caused the majority of the Iroquois to desert the British after 146 years and give their allegiance to the French.

Chapter Seven

A TIME OF PEACE

The records for the period January to August 1757 are muddled to some degree. An after-action report by Capt. Robert Rogers covering a January patrol clarifies much that happened just prior to the March assault on Fort William Henry.

Captain Hobbs apparently died of smallpox in February, as the report refers to his being alive in January. Captain Spikeman was on the patrol with Rogers and although listed as killed, apparently was only wounded and taken prisoner.

Private Thomas Brown, was also listed as killed, was wounded and taken prisoner by the Huron. Although treated roughly, he survived and would later tell what fate had befallen the known prisoners and those listed as missing in action.

Captain Spikeman was slowly butchered by the Huron, scalped and decapitated. The others were stripped, hamstrung and made to run until they dropped and then killed by the Huron.

After the dust had settled from the March attack at Fort William Henry, Lord Loudon, in a realignment of command, assigned the Lake George district to Maj. Gen. Daniel Webb of the British line. This was an unfortunate choice. Loudon knew the importance of the area, as he had headquartered at Fort William Henry from July until November 1756. Then he broke up the division he had with him and went into winter quarters at Albany, New York.

Major General Webb had an excellent record as an administrator and an above average record as a line officer. Unfortunately, at this time he was suffering from hypochondria of an extensive nature with the result that he was inept as a military commander and indecisive as a man.

If the British were having problems, the French were faring no better. Vaudreuil and Montcalm were at each other constantly. This was due in part to the corruption in Vaudreuil's government and in part to Vaudreuil being a native born Canadian. He wanted no interference from the parent government in France. Another problem was that Vaudreuil was under the Department of Marine and Montcalm was Army. Montcalm was quick to damn and took credit for many things for which he should not have. He used French Army regulars sparingly and used the Canadian militia whenever possible. To make matters worse, the British had set up a successful naval blockade of the St. Lawrence River. Canada was short of food, and what promised to be a bumper crop was ripening and would soon need to be harvested.

Montcalm, after considerable debate, allowed himself to be coerced by Vaudreuil into a major assault on Fort William Henry.

Louis Joseph de Montcalm-Gozon, Marquis de Saint-Veran was born in 1712. He was a professional soldier by trade. He fought in the War of the Polish Succession and the War of the Austrian Succession prior to being transferred by the king to New France. He was subordinate to the governor general and felt this created a split command. He repeatedly wrote to France about this and the corruption of the administration, going so far at one time to ask for recall. He was brave and a winner, which the Indians respected. Montcalm was 5'4" tall. When one Indian chief met him, he told Montcalm that he had expected to meet a man as tall as a pine.

He wrote in a letter to his wife that he hoped never to live to see Quebec fall. In other letters he indicated that he felt he would never see her or their children again.

The disaster at Fort William Henry appears to have weighed heavily on his mind. In the battles he fought thereafter he was constantly in the front, exposed to enemy fire. During the battle of Quebec, he rode his horse in front of his advancing troops and received the wound he would die from in a matter of hours. He died before Quebec surrendered. The date was 13 September 1759.

Louis-Joseph, Marquis de Montcalm.
Courtesy *National Archives of Canada*.

Montcalm's second-in-command was Francois Gaston, Duc de Lévis. He was born in 1720 and was a professional soldier. He entered the Army at the age of 15 and distinguished himself in the War of the Austrian Succession. He arrived in Canada in 1756 with Montcalm. After Montcalm's death, he assumed command of the French forces in Canada. He would eventually surrender to the British on the direct order of the governor general. He returned to France and was promoted to lieutenant general in 1761, marshal in 1783 and duke in 1784. He died in 1787.

Montcalm left Montreal in July 1757 with a force of 7,000 regulars and militia and 1,850 Hurons. The force was composed of the battalions of LaSarre, Guienne, Languedoc, LaReine, Bearn and Royal Roussillon, along with *coureurs de bois* and Canadian militia. The Indians were from 40 separate tribes and subtribes, coming from as far west as Wisconsin and Minnesota. They were Tuscaroras, Caughnawagas, Abenaki, Huron, Potawatomie, Ojibway, Miami, Winnebago, Menominee, Shawnee, Mingo, Ottawa, Mohawk, Mohigan, Narragansett, two subtribes of Sioux, Onondaga, Fox, Nascopi, Creek, Nipmucks, Wampanoag, Seneca, Pequot, Illinois, Micmas, Iowa, Oneida, Assiniboia, Delaware, Cayuga, Salk, Algonquin, Penobscot, Montagnais, Shawanoies, Chippewa, Kickapoo, Erie and Arikara. Of the tribes involved, better than 80% had some grievance with the "Anglais."

Arriving at Carillon, Montcalm put his army into camp and proceeded to finalize his attack plans. Two incidents occurred in late July 1757 which, to all appearances, had no marked impression on the British; however, provided the French with needed intelligence. A British patrol of 350 men under the command of New Jersey militia Colonel Parker moved by boat north up Lake George. They apparently landed at Sabbath Day Point, approximately 16 miles north of Fort William Henry and were ambushed by a force of French and Indians that killed 250 of the men and destroyed 24 whaleboats. This occurred on 24 July 1757 and a year later an unknown officer of the 60th Foot would note in a letter to a friend the results of that ambush could still be seen in all its horror. It is a matter of record that Lieutenant Marin, Rogers' French counterpart, attacked a party of woodcutters and their guard at Fort Edward on 23 July 1757.

Colonel Parker's troops were all raw New Jersey militia. Time and distance suggest they met Lieutenant Marin's force on its return to Fort Ticonderoga.

Joseph Marin De La Malgue was born in 1719 in Montreal. He was the son of Lieutenant Colonel Paul Marin De La Malgue of the colonial militia. He entered the army in 1732 and was sent to explore the west. He spent most of the next 13 years in that region. He explored the region around Mackinaw City, Michigan in 1737 and took part in the Chickasaw campaign of 1739-40. In 1740 he made peace and trade agreements with the Sioux in the area west of Green Bay, Wisconsin. In 1745 he took part in the battles in Acadia and at Louisbourg. In 1749 he was again in the west near Ashland, Wisconsin. While there he made peace between the Sioux and Ojibwas and in 1750 was promoted to ensign. In 1751 he was in garrison in Quebec. In 1752 he was back west charged with finding a route to the western sea via the Missouri. He negotiated a truce between the Crees and Sioux. In 1753 he was at the mouth of the Wisconsin River where he stopped a potential quarrel between local Ojibwas and Sioux. He was not successful in finding a route to the western sea, but through his influence was able to ally some 22 tribes with the French.

He returned to Quebec in 1754, traveling to the west again in 1755. In 1756 he was recalled and spent the next two years engaging the British. When he returned he brought with him a large party of Menominee warriors. They would stay and act as his personal scouts. Marin was the French version of Rogers. The two men had a great deal of respect for each other and their units. Their respect was so great that Marin would rescue Israel Putnam, a Ranger officer, from the Huron in 1758. In July 1757, Marin undertook a reconnaissance in the area of Fort Edward. He wiped out a 10-man patrol and a 50-man guard. He was chased for a short distance by a superior force which he held off, losing only three men.

Marin was one of the officers involved in the destruction of Fort Clinton and would personally engage Rogers and the Rangers in 1758. In August of 1756 he engaged a British force of 65 men near Fort William Henry, killing or capturing all but the leader. He was always to be of the opinion that the leader was Rogers, but this is unlikely as Rogers was not at Fort William Henry or Fort Edward at the time.

Marin was promoted to Captain in January 1759 and spent the early part of the year on the Maryland and Pennsylvania frontiers. In the latter part of the year he was captured by the British near Fort Niagara. He would write of his capture, "They announced my capture as a great triumph in their newspaper." His imprisonment was a "horror" and he was finally sent to England and then to France. In 1762 he was once again in Canada, but again became a prisoner of the British in September of that year. He was sent to France and never returned to Canada. In 1773 he was promoted to lieutenant-colonel and died on a military mission to Madagascar in 1774.

The French had little respect for colonial officers, but classed Marin as a colonial officer of great reputation, an aggressive, effective officer. Montcalm would credit Marin with victories, but referred to him as "brave but stupid."

The British had not been idle. In mid-April, Lt. Col. George Monro took command of Fort William Henry. He brought with him two companies of the 35th Foot, a company of Fraser's Highlanders, two companies of the 44th and two companies of the 48th Foot. Major Eyre had done much to clean up the mess the militia had left behind when he and the 44th moved in late in 1756. Colonel Monro would clean up the fort even more. The main force would become the 35th Foot with two companies from the 44th. The 48th returned to Fort Edward and the Frasers were posted elsewhere. Another company of Rangers under Richard Rogers, brother to Robert Rogers, was assigned on a permanent basis. This was based on the fact that the

Rangers were on constant scouts or patrols up the lake and only Captain Spikeman's company was still at Fort William Henry. Circumstantial evidence indicates the commander was Captain Jonathan Ogden. The fort was visited by smallpox in July and Richard Rogers became a victim of the epidemic. Captain Israel Putnam took over as the commander of Richard Rogers' company briefly, returning to Fort Edward by the end of July.

A time of peace.

Strength of Fort W:m Henry, at the time it was attacked, as near as can be now computed.

Six Companies of the 35.th Regiment	510
Detachments of the Royal Americans	100
Independants	100
Massachusetts	800
Jerseys	200
Hampshire	200
Rangers	180
Carpenters & Sailors	60
	2150

Memo from Monro concerning strength of Fort William Henry at time of August 1757 attack. This item is reproduced by permission of *The Huntington Library, San Marino, California.* Loudon Collection, LO4367.

Chapter Eight

SIX DAYS OF PURGATORY

Fort William Henry had been something of a minor nuisance due to uncleanness and changes in construction (suggested and never done). In August 1756 it was visited by James Montressor, chief engineer for His Majesty's Armed Forces in North America, Lieutenant Colonel R. Burton, 48th Foot and William MacLeod, Captain Lieutenant of Artillery. Burton, in a private letter to Lord Loudon, stated that he found smallpox well established, the cleanliness of the fort disgraceful, with garbage and human waste spilling over onto the barracks floors and into the passageways and streets of the fort. He reported, "There are here about 2,500 men, 500 of them sick . . . their camp is nastier than anything I could conceive. Their latrines, kitchens, graves and places for slaughtering cattle are all mixed through their encampment." In all fairness he was speaking not only of the fort, but of the camp as well.

By July 1757 conditions had improved greatly at the fort, although it had just undergone another smallpox epidemic. The regular army was able to maintain discipline to prevent this type of situation. However, the garrison was strengthened with militia who disdained all discipline, would listen only to their own leaders and those not too often. That Colonel Monro was able to maintain any type of discipline and efficiency at all is a credit to his ability as a career army officer.

By 2 August 1757 the fort and camp contained 1,500 military and nonmilitary personnel (excluding women and children). During the night hours of August 2/3 Lieutenant Colonel Young of the 60th Foot arrived with another 1,000 troops, mostly militia.

According to a memo from Colonel Monro, at the time of the assault, there were six companies of the 35th (540 men), a detachment from the 60th or Royal Americans (100 men)

100 independents, 800 Massachusetts militia, 200 Jersey militia, 200 Hampshire militia, 140 Rangers and 60 carpenters and sailors, for a total of 2,140 troops and quasi-troops.

There were over 100 women and an unknown number of children. The army allowed on the average six wives of the enlisted ranks to travel with each company, along with their children. These ladies were of the highest moral fiber and were expected to work as nurses, cooks, hospital help, weavers and on the march as cattle drovers and horse herders. In many regiments they were paid 3-6p per day. They drew stores from the regiment and, if taken ill, were treated, as were their children, either at the local facility hospital or general hospital.

Depending on the duty station, they might have separate quarters in the barracks, a barracks of their own or makeshift shelter. If they were widowed, they were provided with a stipend to get to home and hearth, be it anywhere in the world. Not a few of these ladies were licensed as sutlers. The wives, and to some degree the children, were subject to the King's Articles of War as were their husbands. The majority of dependents at the fort were related to the 35th Foot, and not a few of the militia.

There were provisions at the fort for 6,000 men for six weeks. This does not include shot and powder. These were salt pork which was really raw beef pickled in salt brine given over to mold, worms and worse; hard-tack, readily given to weevils; flour, also given to weevils; and rum or grog for the ranks and brandy for the officers. There were dried vegetables from the fort garden and the fort had a well in the northeast corner dug to water level. There was also a small creek that passed through the camp just west of the fort.

On the morning of 25 July 1757 General Webb, with his staff, left Fort Edward with an escort at 0600 hours. They arrived at Fort William Henry at 1530 hours. This was a planned staff visit. A routine staff inspection was done on the 26th.

A council of war was called 27 July 1757 predicated on the fact that the enemy had been seen in small groups on the west side of the lake, although the major activity had been on the east side of the lake, the French and Indians using Wood Creek as their line of travel. It was known Montcalm had scouts down both sides of the lake.

Notes pertaining to Lieutenant Colonel Monro's queries to General Webb at this meeting give the date at 28 July 1757. Colonel Montressor's journal gives the date as 27 July. The notes give the persons present as Lieutenant Colonel Young, the three engineers, Montressor, Gordon and Williamson, Captain Ord of the artillery train, the Brigade Major Morris and Captain Bartman, the general's aide de camp and the general.

Montressor states the persons present as General Webb, militia colonel, Brevet General Lyman, Major Fletcher, Militia Colonel Glazier, Militia Colonel Angel, Captain Ord, Engineer Colonel Montressor and Engineer Harry Gordon. No mention is made of Lieutenant Colonel Monro. Montressor gives no explanation for this and it is still a mystery.

It does support the fact that there was friction between Lieutenant Colonel Monro and the corps' staff.

Another mystery is who wrote up the following memo concerning the colonel's queries. It was contained within the papers of Colonel Monro to Lord Loudon, but gives no indication as to the writer. The language and phrasing is strongly indicative that the writer was the colonel, after the fact.

Query: In case Fort Edward should be attack'd by the enemy, the signals given & understood of it's being invested, what part am I to act.

Answer: To be sure to march to it's relief, leaving 300 men in the fort as soon as we hear you

	ingage'd, with the enemy, upon the road, we will sent out a strong detachment, to your assistance.
Query:	Whether, of the two forts, is most likely to be attack'd by the enemy? (referring to Fort Edward)
Answer:	That was out of the question, for there was no probability, and hardly a possibility, of their attacking Fort Edward with cannon.
Answer:	If so, I think Fort Wm. Henry ought to have as great a number of men, as can possibly be spar'd, because if they are repuls'd in their attempt, upon Fort Wm. Henry, the affair will be over; but if they take it; I won't say the taking of Fort Edward will be the consequence, but I think, it will be a great step towards it, as they will then have, a road, to bring their cannon. The General said as to the number of men to reinforce Fort Wm. Henry, the most he could spare, was one thousand, one hundred, of them, to be of the RA, before this reinforcement arrived, we had, at Fort Wm. Henry, about 1100 men, fit for duty. The reinforcement of the 1000 men from Fort Edward, were to have been with us, that Saturday to have help'd us, to finish our breastwork but they did not come till it was dark Tuesday night, the next morning being the 3th of August, the enemy attack'd us, and our breast-work, not near finished.

This particular memo was provided, it appears, to Lord Loudon after the battle was over and during the Board of Inquiry.

According to Montressor's journal, the war council decided there were not enough boats to prevent a landing by the French. It was determined it would take 2,000 men to defend the fort, along with an artillery train of two 12-pounders, two 6-pounders, and two 8-pounders. This, in addition to the artillery in place at the fort.

It was also determined that the east bastion had to be raised by one log to prevent clear observation from the rising ground southeast of the fort. This was the second time this observation had been made about the height of the bastions and the walls.

Colonel Montressor issued plans on the 28th day of July for entrenchments and ordered same to be executed.

General Webb and his party departed Fort William Henry for Fort Edward on 29 July. Major Israel Putnam, in charge of the escort party, was ordered to scout ahead. There is no mention in Montressor's journal of Major Putnam seeing any enemy force from a high elevation. That puts to rest one of the existing stories as having no basis in reality. General Webb and his party stopped at a tavern known as "Half Way House," located on the military road between the two forts and moved on to Fort Edward after a brief rest. There exists today a halfway township, but no tavern.

Montressor is not specific in his journal, but sometime after 30 July, General Webb dispatched 1,000 men and some artillery to Fort William Henry under command of Lieutenant Colonel John Young of the 60th Foot. We now know they arrived during the dark of the night on 2/3 August.

If there appears to be a difference between the two memos concerning the council of war, there is. Monro shows there was a great deal of emphasis on "what would happen if Ft. Edward were attacked." Montressor, on the other hand, is somewhat more vague in his statements, again, with only minimal reference to Fort William Henry. This has a basis in that Fort Edward was doing some extensive additions to bolster its defenses and was vulnerable. This apparently made General Webb and his staff somewhat nervous.

This, coupled with what intelligence the Rangers had been bringing into Fort William Henry concerning French movement in the vicinity, was a double negative. The French were on the move, but where and in what strength was unknown. Further, their objective was unknown, leaving all tactical defense measures in limbo. The answers would be forthcoming.

Shortly after Colonel Parker's waterborne patrol was ambushed and annihilated, several smokes were seen quite some distance up the lake.

Captain Putnam and some of his men were sent out to discover the source. They came back in a few hours to report that the enemy was encamped some 16 miles up the lake, roughly the area of Sabbath Day Point. This was 28 July. The Rangers returned up the lake again that night for further scouting. The next day 29 July, General Webb left Fort William Henry. The scouts continued until the night of 2 August, when the Rangers made contact with the enemy.

Thirteen Rangers in two boats left to scout north on Lake George. At about four miles they were ambushed and only five returned about two hours before dawn. The others were either killed or taken prisoner. The garrison at the fort could hear the shots and see the flashes of gunfire, but could do nothing.

Shortly after dawn the enemy appeared on the lake, spreading across the width of the lake in anything that would float. As they approached, they fired on the fort from three floating batteries with no effect as the rounds fell short by half a mile. One of the cannon mounted in the floating batteries is now in display at the fort site. After displaying their strength for some three hours, but never within range of the fort guns, they withdrew to the shelter of Artillery Cove and started landing the troops to join up with the troops using the Indian trail down the west side of the lake. These troops were under the command of the

Marquis de Lévis. The die was cast. As Charles Dickens' Tiny Tim in "A Christmas Carol" would recite roughly a hundred years later, "God bless us, every one."

The story of the battle has been glossed over and, in fact, the truth has been so distorted through the once-over-lightly treatment fiction writers and Hollywood have given this battle, that the story until recently, read as follows, but the actual facts are more riveting. The battle as previously known is presented first.

At dawn on 2 August the Hurons raised the war cry and the attack was on. Some 1,700 British troops who were camped on the elevation to the south of the fort, on what would later be the site of Fort George, barely made it to the fort. They had a 600-yard run. Those who were not fleet of foot or who were too slow in waking never got to the fort. Their tents were burned, and the horses and cattle were run off and slaughtered.

Montcalm's second in command, Marquis de Lévis, used the vacated elevation to establish his base of operations. Montcalm set his base of operations on the west side of the lake just slightly north of the cleared area around the fort. A third contingent was sent to the southeast to blockade the road from Fort Edward. The order of battle was simple. Montcalm would cannonade the fort for a period of time, stop and Lévis would start. While the forts' attention was on Lévis, Montcalm, who had room for mobility, would move his gun emplacements forward. He would start cannonading again and Lévis would stop.

Both men were veterans of the European campaigns and knew that no fort could long stand this type of bombardment. They had 31 cannon, 15 mortars and howitzers. They had the fire power. By steadily moving the cannons forward, they shortened and flattened the arc of the ball, causing a greater impact, eventually forcing a breach. When that happened Montcalm would have the options of using his forces in a mass breaching of the weakened spot or using his regulars for the traditional firing line while his *coureurs de bois* and Hurons forced the breach.

In the interim he used his infantry and sappers to dig new gun emplacements, help move the cannon forward, man sharpshooter pits and picket lines. When not doing this they lazed their time away in camp. Montcalm placed his Hurons in the forest behind him and other than using them for sniping or scouting, kept them confined to the camp area for the duration of the battle. His main concern was a relief column from the south where he knew there were in excess of 4,000 troops. Even with the road blocked he maintained a constant watch to the south.

Montcalm had his artillery in the fort garden and was shelling with heavy artillery from 200 yards. He offered surrender terms (this being the second time) advising that he had made dispositions to render relief impossible. Monro, in sending his reply, sent a young officer who apologized to Montcalm for his untidy appearance and delighted the French officers with the statement, "Not knowing to which tribe of the savages I shall be allotted, I have not known which hair style to wear." Monro's reply was that he and his men would defend themselves to the last. Monro was still hoping for relief.

By the 7th Montcalm was beginning to fret. He was running short of supplies and ammunition. He knew his troops had to get back to Canada to assist with the harvest. He had breached the wall only slightly and the Indians were turning surly. The capture of Webb's messenger, revealing Webb's failure to come to Monro's aid, revived Montcalm's spirits considerably.

Monro, although he had waged an excellent defensive action, was in dire straits. Two sorties had been negative in result, the majority of his cannon had burst from overuse, he was low on shot and powder. His wounded were increasing in number and his medical facilities were not adequate to handle them. The Massachusetts regiment was in a near state of mutiny. They were ready to take their chances with the Hurons rather than go through more artillery barrage. Also, he had he women and children to think of. Lastly, was the ever-present threat of smallpox, the last outbreak having passed only some two or three weeks prior to the attack.

The real story of the battle and subsequent massacre comes from several sources. It is contained in documents and reports as well as letters from the participants. The most extensive is a written report filed in Albany, New York, 2d November 1756 by James Kilby. All that is known of him is that he was at the fort. Some of the information previously recorded was from his report. What follows is from this report as well as other first-hand accounts.

About nine in the morning, the assault became somewhat more personalized as the Indians and Canadians started to appear in the woods around the camp, drawing both small arms and cannon fire from the fort and camp. Fortunately, it had little to no effect due to the distance.

About eleven, the enemy started returning fire at a heavy, steady rate. This lasted for some two hours; when a flag of truce was shown. The officer was conducted to the camp, where he delivered a letter from Montcalm to Monro which was a request for the surrender of the camp and fort.

> *Sir, I have this morning invested your place with a numerous army and superior artillery, and all the savages from the higher parts of the country. The cruelty of which, a detachment of your garrison have lately too much experience. I am obligated in humanity, to desire you to surrender your Fort. I have it yet in my power to restrain the savages, and oblige them to observe a capitulation, as hitherto none of them have been killed, which will not be in my power in other circumstances; and your insisting on defending your Fort, can only retard the loss of it a few days, and must of necessity, expose a unlucky garrison, who can receive no succors considering the*

precautions I have taken. I demand a decisive answer immediately for which purpose I have sent you the Sieur Funtbrunne, one of my aides de camp. You may credit what he will inform you as from me. I am with respect, Sir, your most humble, most obedient servant,
Montcalm.

Monro's answer was to the point.

"Sir, while one log of the Fort, remains upon another, or we have a man to fight, we will defend it."

The French officer returned to his lines and firing started again.

The garrison in the fort consisted of Captain Ormsby of the 35th as well as Lieutenant Good and Ensign Witherington of the 35th, 60 regulars, 150 sailors and carpenters and during the day augmented with provincials to bring the garrison up to 400. Colonel Monro was outside the fort in the camp. This was 3 August.

The British spent the 3rd, 4th, and 5th laying on an artillery barrage of substantial proportions, using grape and canister as well as ball. There was skirmishing on a reasonably steady basis as the Indians and Canadians attempted to penetrate the camp. Losses were minimal for the British, except during the first skirmish, led by provincial Captain Richard Saltonstall, when two provincial officers and 15 provincial privates were lost. Within the fort two mortars burst, leaving them with two 7.5-inch mortars and one howitzer.

The French were persistent and were able to construct a battery under fire which consisted of eight pieces of cannon, 12 and 18-pounders and two 10-inch mortars, at a distance of some 700 yards.

The battery started returning fire on the British at about six in the morning on August 6 – continuing the whole day with little success. The British in the interim had burst a 32-pounder. This may have been located in the northwest bastion and did a fair amount of damage to the interior of the bastion as well as the troops fighting the position.

During the night of 6/7 August, both sides held an artillery duel with a shot being fired about every 15 minutes throughout the night.

In the morning artillery fire became very heavy and lasted until 10:00 A.M. when the French appeared with a flag of truce. The officer was met and desired to speak to Colonel Monro. He was conducted to the fort blindfolded and presented a letter to the colonel, which Montcalm's Indians had taken from the courier they captured. Montcalm hoped by this gesture to show that he chose to carry on the war, like a gentleman. Further, he hoped it might prove demoralizing to the British. It did not.

The letter and other letters between Monro and Webb are given in their original form, next following. It should be remembered that not all of these letters reached Monro, although his seemed to have reached Webb. Included also is Monro's answer to Montcalm.

Lieutenant Colonel Monro's answer to General Montcalm's letter to surrender the fort dated 3 August 1757.

Sir,
The only answer, I can give to your letter, is that I am determined, to defend the Fort, to the last, and I believe it is the resolution, of every man, under my command, I am with the greatest regard.

Sir
Your Most Obedient
& Very Humble Servant
Geo. Monro

Copy of a letter from Colonel Monro to Major General Webb, dated 9 o'clock in the morning, 3 August 1757.

> Sir:
> This is to acquaint you that the enemy are in sight upon the lake, and we know that they have cannon.
> They cut off our two boats between two and three this morning, that were towards our first island. As yet we know nothing of their numbers.
> I am Your Obedient Servant, Geo. Monro, Lt. Col.
> To 35th Regiment.

The following letter was written at about the same time and in the evening, but is incomplete. Again, Colonel Monro was trying to provide accurate intelligence to his superior.

> Sir:
> I send this by three Rangers and shall send you three more in half an hour and continue to do so.
> We have a few men wounded by their random shott, but their body has not yet appeared.
> I believe you will think it proper to send a reinforcement as soon as possible. I can tell you nothing at present, but that I am . . . .

The following letter was written shortly after 6 o'clock in the evening of 3 August.

> Sir:
> This place was so suddenly surrounded by the enemy, that there was no sending off an express. Captain Ogden has three letters of mine to you, which he could not send off hitherto, I hope this one I now write will be sent off tonight.
> General Montcalm sent his aide de camp with a letter to me to surrender the Fort and camp. My

answer was, "that we were determined to defend both the Fort and the Camp to the last," they have not yet erected their batteries, but the Indians have been firing upon us, from the woods all day. Captain Cunningham of the 35th Regiment is wounded in the arm, and a Corporal of the same regiment has had his arm cutt off, and a few men wounded.

I forgot to tell you General Montcalm says in his letter, "he has a numerous army & a superior artillery to ours," I make no doubt....

Letter from Major General Webb to Lieutenant Colonel Monro dated 3 August 1757, 4:30 P.M.

Sir: Your letter General Webb received by the two Rangers of Rogers Company about one o'clock. We have just fired the two minute guns repeated each quarter of an hour to show you we know your situation, but as for determining any further the general cannot, till he has more particulars or intelligence from you which he desires you will take every opportunity of giving him. The signalls would have been answered early in the morning, but that nobody who heard them could give a proper account how they were fixed, and soon after they became promiscuous. Six Rangers were sent off to you to inquire into your situation and acquaint us wherewith and whether the communication was cut off between the two forts. The general doubts not but everything will be done for the best on your's and Colonel Young's part and is determined to assist you as soon as possible with the whole army if required. We have as yet no alarm here from the enemy. This goes by three of Putnams' Rangers with orders to destroy it if likely to be taken.

I am G. Bartman,
Aid de Camp

Letter from Major General Webb to Lieutenant Colonel Monro, 4 August 1757, 12 noon. The letter was intercepted by the French and sent to Colonel Monro during the morning of 7 August 1757.

> *Sir, I am directed by General Webb to acknowledge the receipt of three of your letters, two bearing date about nine yesterday morning and one about six in the evening by two Rangers, which are the only men that have got in here except two yesterday morning with your first, acquainting him of the enemy being in sight. He has ordered me to acquaint you he does not think it prudent as you know his strength at this place, to attempt a junction or to join you till reinforced by the militia of the colonies, for the march of which repeated requests have been sent. One of our scouts brought in a Canadian prisoner last night from the investing party, which is very large and have peopled all the grounds five miles on this side of Fort Wm. Henry. The number of the enemy is very considerable, the prisoner says seven thousand, and have a large train of artillery, with mortars, and were to open their batteries this day. The General thought proper to give you this intelligence, that in case he should be so unfortunate from the delay of the militia not to have it in his power to give you timely assistance you might be able to make the best terms as were left in your power. The bearer is a Sergeant of the Connecticut Forces and if is happy enough to get in will bring advices from you. We keep continual scouts going to endeavor to get in or bring intelligence from you.*
> *I am &c.*
G. Bartman, Aide de Camp

Letter from Lieutenant Colonel Monro to Major General Webb, 4 August 1757.

> *Sir: I can as yet tell you very little more than I did in my last of the enemys investing us. I presume you*

*got my letter acquainting you with General
Montcalm's letter to me, modestly advising to
surrender.—We are continually harassed with the
Indians all round us, & we have had both officers and
men wounded by them. We have seen of their regulars
but not within shott of us. We believe they are
employed in erecting batteries. And as we are very
certain that part of the enemy have got between you
and us up on the high road, would therefore be glad if
it meets with your approbation, the whole army was
marched. You may depend upon Colonel Young and
me doing our part as far as lyes in our power and we
join in compliments to you.*
I am &c., Geo. Monro

Letter from Major General Webb to Lieutenant Colonel Monro, 6 August 1757. Received during the night of 9 August 1757.

*Sir: Your's of this morning 6 o'clock, we have
received, and I am directed by General Webb to
acquaint you that as we have now got together by the
march of the militia in the highest spirits, three armies
of five thousand men in different parts of the woods,
we shall vett out in the night with the whole joined
together and make no doubt of cutting the enemy
entirely off.*
I am &c., G. Bartman, Aide de Camp

We shall bring a field train.

*The bearer if pursued, is ordered to make away
with the letter.*

Letter from Lieutenant Colonel Monro to Major General Webb, morning 6 August 1757.

*Sir: As a proof of the insufficiency of the artillery,
we have had within 24 hours, two 10-pounders, one*

12-pounder and one mortar burst, from which you will see the necessity of sending up a fresh supply of artillery as soon as possible. We have been obliged to give two 12-pounders from the camp, which we could very ill spare. In case my letter of this morning should not have reached you, I am to report to you, that the enemy are playing upon us from a battery of nine pieces of cannon, mostly 10 and 12-pounders.

I am &c., Geo. Monro

Letter from Lieutenant Colonel Monro to Major General Webb, 6 August 1757, 6:00 P.M.

Sir: This is the third letter I wrote to you this day. In my two former I acquainted you with the situation we were then in. Since that time, there is another gun in the fort rendered useless by the enemy's fire, and we have discovered new works carrying on which we believe will be completed this evening or tomorrow morning, which will bear equally upon the fort and upon the camp. I beg pardon for saying that if the reinforcement we had reason to expect from your letter, the only one I have ever received from you, which bears date August 3, had arrived in time, our situation probably would have been better. About two o'clock afternoon this day, I received from you a verbal message by two Rangers mentioning an expectation you had of being joined by Sir Wm. Johnson and some Indians. As they delivered it in so confused a manner, I really could not rightly understand it. I have as frequently as possible acquainted you with every circumstance that has passed since the enemy's appearance and therefore submit the whole to your better judgment. In my former letters of this day, I told you there were four cannon burst in the fort within 24 hours and likewise I had made a request of a fresh supply of artillery having sent into the fort two 12-pounders which we have spare very ill from this camp.

I am &c., Geo. Monro

Letter from Major General Webb to Lieutenant Colonel Monro, 8 August 1757, 6:00 P.M. Intercepted by the French during the evening of 9 August 1757.

Sir: I am directed by General Webb to acquaint you that it is entirely owing to the delay of the militia that he has not yet moved up to your assistance, but as he has now got a part of them and expects a thousand more tomorrow, you may depend upon their arrival, that he will not fail to march to your assistance. You will upon hearing him engaged, consult with Colonel Young how you can by making a vigorous sally from the camp, best support his attack. We have sent you repeated letters, but are sorry only one has go in, tho we hope, none have fallen into the enemys hands, as most of the parties have returned, but were all closely pursued. We shall have about one hundred and fifty Indians with Sir Wm. Johnson, but shall keep them nigh on to prevent any mistake. We wish most heartily that you may be able to hold out a little longer, and hope soon to have it in our power to relieve you from your present disagreeable situation, tho we are informed by a prisoner we took the first evening of the enemy's landing, that they are seven thousand strong. On receipt of this, the General desires you will send off several intelligences to acquaint him thereof, likewise what you judge the enemys numbers to be, and how long you think you could hold out against the present cannonading.
      I am &c., G. Bartman, Aid de Camp

Letter from Lieutenant Colonel Monro to Major General Webb, 8 August 1757, AM.

Sir: The fort and camp will hold out in hopes of the speedy relief from you which we hourly expect, and if that does not happen, we must fall into the hands of our enemies. Your letter dated 4th instant was delivered to me by an Aid de Camp of General

> Montcalm's. That latter falling into his hands was a very unhappy thing and has to be sure, elevated him greatly. As to the numbers of the enemy, the Canadian prisoner mentioned to you, every body here is of opinion that was greatly magnified. If they really had those numbers, they might have demolished us at once, with out loss of time. The enemy are constantly playing upon us from two batteries of nine pieces cannon. Relief is greatly wanted.
>
> I am, &c., Geo. Monro

Colonel Monro's August 3 letter to Montcalm, in which he was resolved to defend the fort to the last, had the effect of lifting the troops' spirits, and no thought was given to surrender until it was impossible to hold the fort any longer. Further, the messenger from Montcalm had also delivered the compliments of the French artillery commander, Lieutenant Colonel Francois Le Mercier to Mr. Collins who commanded the British artillery, for performing his job so well; which also lifted the spirits of the troops. Quite frankly, it would appear that not only was there one battery of regular army artillery, but the sailors at the fort were manning the artillery as well. As they were considered to be the finest gunners in the world at that time, it is no small wonder the French were duly impressed by the British cannon fire.

On the 6th and 7th the British had another 32-pounder as well as two 18-pounders and one 12-pounder burst. One brass 6-pounder was destroyed by a direct hit by the French. This left the British with one 12-pounder, two 9-pounders, four 4-pounders, one howitzer and one mortar and the mortar burst on the 7th.

The French had the battery mentioned earlier as well as another of 10 cannons, one mortar and two howitzers, which were put into action on the 6th. By the 8th, it was evident the French were entrenching another battery about a hundred yards away.

Copy of a letter from Lt. Colonel Monro to Major Gen. Webb. Dated Fort Wm. Henry Monday Morning the 8 Augt. 1757.

Sir,

The Fort I am pretty well satisfied cannot hold out much longer. We must be forced by Great want of Rest &c. if that does not happen, the enemy Fire into the Hands of our Enemies. ——— Your letter states that he'd without my desiring to do he by an aid de camp of General Montcalm I. Montcalm falling into his hands, who are very unhappy when Canada has is to be very elated with success. —— As is the numbers of the enemy, the Canadians & Indians Sebastian & you were fifty here in Garrison, ne a Sixteen Thousand, — Why really had there been but, my only hope is absolutely at once withdraw from home. The enemy are Cannonading us from two Batteries of Roadpieces of Canon each. Believe me

I am &c.
Gen. Monro

"Relief is greatly wanted." Copy of a letter from Lt. Colonel Monro to Major Gen. Webb.
Dated Fort Wm. Henry, Monday Morning the 8th Aug. 1757. This item is reproduced by permission of
The Huntington Library, San Marino, California. Loudon Collection, LO4041.

The fighting was brisk on the 8th, with the British forces doing everything within their power to annoy the French and Indian forces just outside the camp's line of resistance. During the evening of the 8th an engineer (Adam Williamson) surveyed the fort and it was determined that the fort had sustained very little damage from the French artillery. However, the British were very short on ammunition and powder and the other stores had been damaged to some extent. Although not mentioned by this source, it is known that medical supplies were almost totally depleted. Further, the men had been without rest for five nights and were almost stupefied.

The defense was continued throughout the night of the 8th and the French could be heard at work at the back of the garden.

The British were down to basically small arms, although they were able to fire grape shot at the French with some regularity. The French were laying on artillery with a fair degree of accuracy on the camp, not forgetting the fort. The damage was minimal.

By morning on the 9th, the French had just about completed two more batteries, one for bombs and the other for cannon. The British felt the batteries would open fire on the 10th and with that the French would gain the ditch and it would all be over.

Fighting was heavy during the morning of the 9th, until about 9 o'clock. After consultation of all the officers in the camp and fort, the British showed a white flag. At that point all firing on both sides came to a stop. Lieutenant Colonel John Young, although wounded, went to the French in order to obtain a capitulation. This took until one o'clock in the afternoon.

Using a direct quote, "While this affair was on the Carpet," the Indians came about the fort and with great tranquility led off all the horses they could find without taking any notice of the British troops.

The capitulation read as follows:

Articles of capitulation granted to Lieutenant-Colonel Monro for his Britannic Majesty's garrison at Fort William Henry, the entrenched camps adjoining the same and their dependencies, by the Marquis de Montcalm, General of his Most Christian Majesty's troops in Canada, the 9th of August, 1757.

Article 1st

The garrison of Fort William Henry, and the troops in the entrenched camp adjoining, shall march out with arms, and other honors of war.

The baggage of the officers and of the soldiers only.

They shall proceed to Fort Edward escorted by a detachment of French troops and some officers and interpreters attached to the Indians, at an early hour tomorrow morning.

Article 2d

The gate of the Fort shall be delivered up to the troops of his Most Christian Majesty after the signing of the capitulation and the entrenched camp, on the departure of his Britannic Majesty's troops.

Article 3d

All the artillery, warlike stores, provisions and in general everything except the effects of the officers and soldiers specified in the first article, shall upon honor, be delivered up to the troops of his Most Christian Majesty, and with that view an exact inventory of the property herein mentioned shall be delivered after the capitulation, observing that this Article includes the fort, entrenchment and dependencies.

Article 4th

The garrison of the fort, entrenched camp and dependencies shall not be at liberty to serve for eighteen months, reckoning from this date, against his Most Christian Majesty, nor against his allies; with the capitulation, shall furnish an exact return of his troops, wherein shall be set forth the names of the officers, Majors, other officers, Engineers, artillery officers, Commissaries and employees.

Article 5th

All the officers, soldiers, Canadians, women and Indians, taken on land since the commencement of this war in North America, shall be delivered at Carillon within the space of three months, on the receipts of the French Commandant, to whom they shall be delivered; an equal number of the garrison of Fort George (the French name for Fort William Henry) shall be at liberty to serve, according to the return which shall be given in thereof by the English officer, who will have charge of the prisoners.

Article 6th

An officer shall be given as a hostage until the return of the detachment, which will be furnished as an escort for his Britannic Majesty's troops.

Article 7th

All the sick and wounded who are not in a condition to be removed to Fort Edward, shall remain under the protection of the Marquis de Montcalm, who will take proper care of them and return them immediately after they are cured.

Article 8th

Provisions for the subsistence of said troops shall be issued for this day and tomorrow only.

Article 9th

The Marquis de Montcalm being willing to show Lieutenant Colonel Monro and his garrison some token of his esteem on account of their honorable defense, grants them one piece of cannon – a six pounder.

Done at noon, in the trenches before Fort William Henry, the ninth of August, one thousand seven hundred and fifty seven.

/s/ Geo. Monro, Lieutenant Colonel, 35th and Commandant of his Majesty's forces in and near Fort William Henry.

Granted in the name of his Most Christian Majesty, pursuant to the power I possess from marquis de Vaudreuil, his Governor and Lieutenant General in New France.

/s/ Montcalm

As to the honoring of the Articles of Capitulation, what follows is quoted directly from Kilby's memorial.

No sooner were the savages acquainted, the capitulation was concluded, but they began to help, and crowd about the fort, the camp, and the road between them eyeing the passengers backwards and forwards, very narrowly; but contented themselves at first, with Howd'ye Brother and picking his pocket, but it was not long before they play'd at higher games.

The Fort garrison was ordered over to the camp; and permitted to carry what baggage they could; which was not altogether unnoticed by the Indians; for they laugh'd and made considerable fun of us as we march'd along, well knowing, the property of our packs, would remain with us but a very short time. Before we got out of the fort, the savages scaled the walls and came in, running about, searching every nook and corner of the fort; where we left them to pursue what methods they thought proper; and what afforded them much satisfaction, was, the murder of the sick and wounded in the hospital; which was in agitation, when the rear of the garrison was marching out.

A French missionary named Roubaud wrote, "I saw one of these barbarians come out of the case mates with a human head in his hand, from which the blood ran in streams, and which he paraded as if he had got the finest prize in the world."

In a memorandum apparently written for the Board of Inquiry in Albany after the battle, Colonel Monro had little to say about the militia during the battle.

The Massachusetts people consisting of 800 men declared to Colonel Fry; very early the morning of the capitulation that they were quite wore out, and would stay no longer and that they would rather be knock'd in the head by the enemy as stay to parish behind the breastwork; till that time, they behav'd and did their duty better than either the Jersey or Hampshire men, who could never be brought to do their duty, with regularity or resolution.

The Provincials in the fort behav'd scandalously when they were to fire over the parapet, they lay down upon their faces and fir'd straight up in the air. I sent orders to the Captain who commanded in the fort to take the first man, that behav'd in that manner and hang him over the wall to be shot at by the enemy.

That Colonel Monro had a high regard for the regulars was also evidenced in the same memo. He wrote as follows:

No man could behave with more coolness and resolution then the 6 companies of the 35th Regiment, both within the breastwork and the fort.

During the early afternoon of the 9th, Montcalm came to the British camp to settle the time and order of march from Fort William Henry to Fort Edward. He personally felt the proper time would be between 10 and 11 that night. When questioned as to escort he indicated 100 men from the

Regiment of Bearn, 100 men from the Regiment Languedoc and a Brigade of Marines, a total of 500 men. He further indicated that if the British felt that an insufficient number he would provide as many men as they felt was proper. He took his leave, promising to return some two hours before departure to make sure everything that was in his power to do to provide for their safety had been done.

The British started to prepare for the move. Montcalm very shortly returned and advised that upon thinking about the planned march and remembering what had happened at Fort Oswego when the French moved prisoners before the passions of the Indians had died down; he now felt the British should stay the night as the Indians were full of wrath.

It would be learned later in an after-the-fact fashion that following Montcalm's return to his camp the second time that the Hurons approached him with the story that General Johnson was approaching with his Indians to assist the fort. This was a story of their own invention. It also proves just how devious, ingenious and bloodthirsty they were. Their hope was that Montcalm would break the capitulation, thereby sacrificing the British to the whims of the Huron.

Montcalm instead issued orders before sunset that the British should make ready to march at midnight. The British, with a great deal of silence, got under arms and prepared to move at midnight. The grenadier company of the Otways (35th) marched out of line and went forward some two to three hundred yards and halted for about an hour. No escort joined. Instead a single Frenchman came and informed Captain Trice, their commander, that General Montcalm had changed his mind in regards to their departure. This was based on the fact that he had gone to the Indian camp and found that fully two-thirds of them were missing. He suspected that they had set up an ambush along the road and he felt daylight would be better for their departure.

The British spent a disagreeable night in camp under the protection of a hundred French regulars and at daybreak got up and prepared for the much wished departure.

As to the young British officer who apologized to the French for the state of his hair, no mention is ever made.

Another source of information concerning the battle is the journal of Colonel James Montressor, chief engineer in the provinces. The journal dates from April 1757 to well after the battle and subsequent massacre. He was witness to the battle, but from a distance of roughly 16 miles at Fort Edward. Colonel James Gabriel Montressor was born in St. James, Westminster, London in 1705. He saw service at Gibraltar and upon reaching the grade of colonel was the second engineer in England. He saw service in America from late 1755 to 1760. He died 6 January 1776, in Teynham, Kent, England.

What follows is an annotated transcript of his journal, covering the period 1 July to 16 August 1757.

According to the journal, the British knew of the French buildup as early as 1 July. Captain Israel Putnam, the pugnacious Ranger, was in an ambush position at South Bay, Lake Champlain on that date. A party of Hurons estimated at 200-300 in strength came within range. The Rangers fired, wounding and killing several. The Hurons landed, attempted to surround the Rangers and walked into a second volley after which Captain Putnam made a tactical withdrawal.

General Webb, upon receipt of Major Putnam's message about the ambush, dispatched General Lyman and Ensign Brown with 36 members of the Otways (35th) and 300 others as a screening party. Major Putnam came into Fort Edward the night of 1 July having left 15 men to protect three wounded. It was never noted if the 18 made it to Fort Edward.

On 3 July, four German deserters came into Fort Edward from Fort Carillon. Interrogation developed that Montcalm was in Montreal planning a march to Carillon with the battalions of Languedoc, LaSarre, Bearn and Rousillon (all regular army), 150 marines and 500 Indians and 500 Canadians *(coureurs de bois)*. He was bringing cannon and mortar from Canada and Crown Point, and would have some 80 cannon and an unknown number of mortars for his attack. There was no mention of the locus of the attack.

General Lyman returned to Fort Edward on 4 July not having seen any Huron. He did find the scalped and badly mutilated body of one of Major Putnam's men.

During the late evening hours of 6 July a Rhode Island militiaman on his way back from the latrine was accosted by a French officer within the picket lines of Fort Edward. The officer asked about the number of personnel and artillery at Fort Edward. He first offered money and then threatened him. The trooper pointed out that all he had to do was yell and help was at hand. The officer left. From the description of the officers's uniform, this was in all likelihood Lieutenant Marin, Robert Rogers' French counterpart.

On Sunday 10 July, General Johnson's Mohawks brought in a French prisoner from Crown Point. Interrogation developed that Montcalm was moving south with six battalions, 300 vessels and all the cannon taken on the Ohio and at Oswego.

A dispatch arrived at Fort Edward from Fort William Henry on 11 July advising that a party from the fort had been ambushed by an estimated 200 enemy and retreated to the fort with the loss of several personnel and a lieutenant killed.

It was quiet until 21 July when a Ranger from a party of 40 Rangers and one lieutenant came into Fort Edward. He reported an ambush near South Bay. The lieutenant and three others were killed. The balance of the party returned before the day was over.

A message from Fort William Henry was received that day advising that Captain McGinnis and two of his party wounded and had killed four of the enemy. He was still on patrol.

Fort Edward received the attention of the French and Indians on 23 July. A party of woodcutters and their protective screen were attacked. The result was several wounded, plus several killed and scalped, including a sergeant, a corporal and ten others. Captain Putnam went in pursuit and reported back the next day and there was a large encampment near the remains of old Fort Anne consisting of an estimated 500-600 men.

A message from Fort William Henry on the 24th of July advised that New Jersey Militia Colonel Parker had gone on a waterborne patrol toward Fort Carillon with some 300 men. They had been attacked by French and Indians from both water and land. They lost several officers and 250 of the 300 men in the patrol as well as 24 whaleboats.

On the morning of 25 July, General Webb and his staff and Colonel Montressor left Fort Edward with an escort at 0600 hours proceeding to Fort William Henry, arriving at 1530 hours. This was a planned staff visit. A routine inspection was done on the 26th.

A council of war was called on the 27th of July, predicated on the fact that the enemy had been seen in small groups on the west side of the lake, although the major activity had been on the east side of the lake, the French and Indians using Wood Creek as their line of travel. It was known Montcalm had scouts down both sides of the lake. What was not known at the time was that Lévis and his troops were using the old Indian trail on the west side of the lake to move down to Sabbath Day Point to make junction with Montcalm's waterborne force.

Those at the meeting were Major General Webb, Militia Colonel-Brevet General Lyman, Major Fletcher, Militia Colonel Glazier, Militia Colonel Angel, Captain Ord, Engineer Colonel Montressor, and Engineer Harry Gordon. Missing was Lieutenant Colonel Monro, Commander of Fort William Henry. Montressor gives no explanation for this and it is still a mystery. It does reinforce the obvious differences between the general and the colonel.

The council decided there were not enough boats to prevent a landing by the French. It was determined it would take 2,000 men to defend the fort, along with an artillery train of two 12-pounders, two 6-pounders, and two 8-pounders. This appears to have been in addition to the artillery in place at the fort.

It was also determined that the east bastion had to be raised by one log to prevent clear observation from the rising ground southeast of the fort. This was the second time this observation had been made about the height of the bastions and walls.

Colonel Montressor issued plans on the 28th of July for entrenchments and ordered same to be executed.

General Webb and his party departed Fort William Henry for Fort Edward on 29 July. Major Putnam in charge of the escort party was ordered to scout ahead.

Webb and his party stopped at a tavern known as "Half Way House," located on the military road between the two forts. They moved on shortly after a brief rest.

Montresssor is not specific in his journal, but sometime between 30 July and 1 August, General Webb dispatched 1,000 men and some artillery to Fort William Henry under command of Colonel Young.

Nothing appears in the journal until 4 August when Montressor notes a messenger arrived from Fort William Henry appraising General Webb of the attack. Colonel Monro clearly and politely stated the situation and asked for help. Montressor's journal reflects only that the note appraised of the attack. Webb sat on his hands and finally sent the response which resulted in the eventual surrender of the fort.

General Webb definitely knew of the attack and siege by 3 August. Two Rangers brought in a French deserter on that date. The deserter advised that the French had some 300 boats, a large artillery train, 4,000 militia, 4,500 Indians, 4,000 Canadians (*coureurs de bois*) and 3,500 regulars and had invested the fort.

This confirmed a report by other Rangers that at 0500 hours that morning they counted some 300 boats on Lake George. That number of boats would have been unusual enough, but the boats were planked together by twos and carrying cannon. They were firing on the fort with no apparent effect as the range was too great.

Two men from Fort William Henry came in on 3 August. They had been out on patrol. They reported a large encampment on the west side of Lake George about six miles from Fort William Henry, or approximately in the vicinity of what is now Bolton's Landing, although the area was never named. They had also seen the Otways (35th) pull back into the fort.

The report of the camp is at odds to what is known. The French were camped almost on top of Fort William Henry, within a mile. As to the second report, it was confirmed later at the Board of Inquiry into the loss of the fort that Colonel Monro put out a skirmish line to penetrate the French positions on two occasions and failed both times.

General Webb called a staff meeting at Fort Edward on 5 August. Attending were Colonel Lyman, Major Fletcher, Colonel Glazier, Colonel Angel, Captain Ord, Engineer Montressor and Engineer Gordon. Three questions were raised by the general.

    1. In view of the information received from a captured French lieutenant and the patrols; was it practicable to go to the assistance of Fort William Henry? There was no question but what Colonel Monro's message of the 4th added emphasis to the situation.

    ANSWER: Not practicable.

    2. That given the enemys' estimated strength and Fort Edward's present situation (having additional construction done); was it proper to remain at Fort Edward?

    ANSWER: That it was proper to retreat and meet up with militia known to be on the way in response to Webb's messages and make a stand as soon as possible.

    3. In case of a retreat from Fort Edward was it proper to leave a holding force?

    No answer was ever given for his question.

As the meeting broke up, General Webb directed his staff to keep themselves ready to march at a minute's warning and that if there was any carriage it should be divided as equally as possible.

Militia from Albany and Schenectady estimated at 1,500 strong arrived at Fort Edward on 6 August along with Sir William Johnson and his Mohawks. Montressor noted that the individual cannon shots from both sides engaging each other at Fort William Henry could be heard and counted.

On 7 August, Montressor asked for any changes to orders as issued by Webb on the 5th and there were none.

At approximately 2000 hours on the 9th of August, a man who had escaped from Fort William Henry came into Fort Edward and advised that Fort William Henry had capitulated at 0700 hours that morning.

Sometime during the day of 10 August, two French officers who had deserted Montcalm at Fort William Henry came into Fort Edward. They advised some of the fort personnel did get escort, but they were at the head of the column. A detachment was sent out from Fort Edward to escort them. The personnel from Fort William Henry consisted of three officers and the color bearers. General Webb ordered out a relief force under Major Putnam. Indications are that it was an all Ranger force. It would arrive at Fort William Henry on the 11th.

On 11 August, smoke from the burning Fort William Henry could be seen at Fort Edward. More French deserters arrived at Fort Edward. They indicated that Montcalm had the fort burned and the Hurons were not happy. Colonel Frye of the Massachusetts militia and Captain MacLeod came into Fort Edward.

Montressor notes that on 16 August, the last of the survivors arrived at Fort Edward. The day also saw a general court martial for a lieutenant of the Massachusetts militia for inciting desertion. The results were not noted.

French dispositions during the battle have been misleading to a degree. It was originally thought that all the

French forces had come by boat from Carillon. The force was divided. Montcalm brought part of the force by boat and Marquis de Lévis brought his troops over land by way of the Indian trail down the west side of Lake George. To add to the confusion, a French map shows Lévis encamped at the redoubt the British had on the south side of Camp William Henry.

The displacement of the French was such that Montcalm was west of the fort and Lévis was actually located unperceived by the British with some 2,500 men in the woods south of the fort. It was also thought that the French had only a skirmish line across the road to Fort Edward. In fact, the skirmish line was composed of some 1,500 French and Indians dispersed to the depth of five miles from Fort William Henry toward Fort Edward. These were under the command of a French officer known as LaCorne.

In clarification of the layout of Camp William Henry and the fort, the map of 1756 (see p. 33) gives basically the camp's main line of resistance as it was then. By 1757, the camp had extended south of the fort some 600 yards, with the main redoubt being at that point, with breastworks along the main line of resistance to the western side of the camp. Later maps are deceptive in appearance, showing redoubts where there were none and in one instance, reflecting the Marquis de Lévis' camp as a redoubt for the fort. The main line of resistance to the west was some 400 yards from the west wall of the fort. The line from the redoubt on the south of the fort to the westernmost breastworks ran at an angle from south to northwest. The north was covered by the fort proper as was the marsh to the east.

Chapter Nine

CAPTURE WAS WORSE THAN DEATH

It would be crass to attempt to put thoughts into a dead person's mouth. It can be presumed from what knowledge we have, that death was far more preferable to being taken alive by the Indians. Capture by the French was uncomfortable, but you survived. Some Indian prisoners did survive either through sheer willpower or by "playing dumb," for lack of a better term. These were usually adopted into a tribe and waited until they could escape. Most were not that lucky.

Navy Lieutenant Charles Spendelow, in his journal entries about his time with Braddock, wrote of a ten-year-old child the troops found standing in a stream. The child had two holes in his head and had been scalped. The Army doctors tried to save the child, but he died within 10 days.

Colonel Montressor mentioned in his journal that the scalped and badly mutilated body of one of the Rangers had been found by one of the patrols from Fort Edward.

Private Brown of the Rangers told of seeing captives being hamstrung and made to run until they could no longer run and then being killed and scalped – not necessarily in that order.

Kenneth Roberts in his book, "Northwest Passage," told of men having strips of flesh cut from their stomachs and used to hang them from a broken tree branch while their ribs were cut from their bodies one at a time.

In another instance, and indeed probably more than one, prisoners were forced to watch while a friend or fellow prisoner was flayed alive and made to eat his own flesh, raw and cooked. The others were forced to eat his flesh or join his agony.

Sometimes the prisoner was just scalped and if he or she survived, the Indians would dump glowing embers or burning sand on the stripped skull.

Necklaces of red hot hatchet blades were hung around the victims' necks. Swords, musket barrels or any metal would be heated in fire and seared across the victims' tenderest parts. Finger nails were pulled out and hot embers pressed into the wound. When it festered, the swelling was bitten out and veins pulled out and seared. Sinews were cut at the wrist and ankle and wound out on sticks.

There are recorded instances of the Indians' play. Two priests were taken prisoner. The elder one went through seven hours of torture and was scalped alive. The younger was covered with pitch from head to toe and then set on fire. The fire was then repeatedly put out by boiling hot water only to be relit. This lasted for 17 hours until he died. In another the prisoner was turned into a pin cushion by having pine splinters forced into his skin. A fire was built around him and he was burned alive. Two others were thrown into a fire and held with pitchforks, that the Indians had looted, until they expired. The gauntlet was the least of their games.

The known descriptions and accounts of what the Indians could do, if so disposed, are numerous and need not be repeated again.

In perspective, the white man was really no better in his treatment of the Indian. Quarter by either side was never expected and rarely given. A word of caution, should you feel smug and safe in the modern world of the 1990's. Read your newspaper, news magazines, and watch television. Only the date has changed.

Chapter Ten

A DAY IN HELL

After a night guarded by a hundred French regulars, left to their own thoughts, the British stirred anew at the break of dawn wanting to get underway to Fort Edward.

As it lightened, the British saw the Indians in vast numbers surrounding the camp and priming their weapons. At that point it was evident that what they had been through the previous six days was but a foreshadowing of things to come.

The first thing the Indians did was plunder the heavy baggage and then they deprived the soldiers of their individual gear. They became so enraged when anyone resisted that Colonel Monro gave the order for the men to put down their individual bags. They turned on the sick and wounded in the tents in the camp to hack and butcher them in front of the other troops which, according to Kilby, "terrified us to the greatest degree imaginable."

Another witness with a sick sense of humor described in his diary how the Indian doctors proceeded to cure the sick and wounded with their tomahawks. They took possession of swords, watches, hats and coats. They even tore the shirts from the backs of officers and soldiers before finally scalping their owners.

They then turned on the officers and soldiers, carrying some of them just outside the camp lines. They were particularly brutal to the Indians and Negroes in the militia whom they immediately cut to pieces, while others they took off as prisoners, most never to be seen again. The Negroes were not slaves, but rather they were freemen who chose to fight for their country. It cost them, as it would so many others, their lives.

Kilby commented, ". . . upon complaining of the barbarous treatment, we were informed it could not be remedied, which made us wish ourselves in the same situation we were in before capitulation; thinking to fight as long as we could and at last die like soldiers, preferable to the shocking brutality wherewith the savages treated us."

Father Pierre Roubaud, whom we referred to earlier, would prove to be one of the few French to help the British that day. After the war he would attempt to recoup the money he spent to ransom the prisoners from the Indians, but was never able to recover the money from either the French or British. He would in later years leave the priesthood, return to France, get married, open a bakery and after his wife's death, join a monastery outside of Paris where he lived out his life.

Father Roubaud saved the life of the only child and woman to survive the massacre. A Huron was threatening to kill the child when the mother saw Father Roubaud. She rushed to him pleading for help. He learned the Huron wanted the scalp. The father talked another Huron out of a scalp, gave it in exchange for the baby and took the mother and child to the protection of Montcalm's tent. Before the war was over he would ransom some 103 persons from the Huron.

Other witness accounts, as reported in the papers, indicated, "The throats of most, if not all, the women were cut, their bellies ripped open, their bowels taken out and thrown upon the faces of the dead and dying bodies; and the children were taken by the heels and their brains beat out against the trees and stones."

A survivor by the name of Carver told how he was seized by three or four Hurons who threatened him with their tomahawks and started tearing his clothing from his body. He asked a French soldier for protection. The Frenchman called him an "English dog" and pushed him back to the Indians. The Hurons started to drag Carver to a nearby swamp when an English officer stripped of all but his pantaloons ran by. One of Carver's capturers jumped on the officer but was thrown off. The other Hurons engaged with Carver left him and one of them sank his tomahawk into the officer's back. Carver started to run for cover of the surrounding forest and was joined by a boy of about 12 years of age. The boy begged protection. They ran together for a short distance and the boy was finally dragged from him by the Hurons. Carver stated that from the boy's screams he was apparently scalped alive.

Confusion was so great at one point 80 men from the New Hampshire militia were captured in a group and butchered immediately.

Colonel Frye of the Massachusetts militia described the massacre in his diary as follows:

> ... *Wednesday, 10th August*
> *Early this morning we were ordered to prepare for our march, but found the Indians in a worse temper (if possible) than last night, every one having a tomahawk, hatchet, or some other instrument of death, and constantly plundering from the officers their arms & ca.;* [sic] *this Col Munro complained of, as a breach of the Articles of Capitulation, but to no effect; the French officers however told us that if we would give up the baggage of the officers and men to the Indians they thought it would make them easy, which at last Col Munro consented to; but this was no sooner done than they began to take the Officers' hats, swords, guns and cloaths, stripping them all to their shirts, and on some officers left no shirt at all. While this was doing they killed and scalp'd all the sick and wounded before our faces, and then took them out from our troops all the Indians and Negroes and carried them off; one of the former they burnt alive afterwards.*
> *At last with great difficulty the troops got from the Retrenchment, but they were no sooner out than the savages fell upon the rear, killing and scalping, which occasioned an order for a halt, done in great confusion at last, but, as soon as those in the front knew what was doing in the rear they again pressed forward, and thus the confusion continued & encreased till we came to the advanced guard of the French, the savages still carrying away Officers, privates, women and*

> children, some of which later they kill'd & scalpt in the road. This horrid scene of blood and slaughter obliged our officers to apply to the French Guard for protection, which they refus'd & told them they must take to the woods and shift for themselves, which many did, and in all probability many perish't in the woods; many got into Fort Edward that day and others daily continued coming in, but vastly fatigued with their former hardships added to this last, which threw several of them into deliriums . . .

Colonel Frye related his own experience in a letter to Thomas Hubbard, Speaker of the House of Representatives of Massachusetts.

> . . . I was strip'd myself of my arms & cloathing, that I had nothing left but briches stockings shoes & shirt; the Indians round me with their tomahawks spears, etc., threatening death I flew to the Officers of the French Guards for protection but they would afford me none, therefore was oblig'd to fly and was in the woods till the 12th, in the morning of which I arriv'd at Fort Edward almost famished . . .

Kilby's journal referring again to the massacre, is both understated and pointed.

> . . . things were running to extremes, when one of the companies pushed out of the line, another followed, and so on till the greatest part was out. . . . It was strange to see that the men, who but the morning before, pursued these savages into the very woods, upon this occasion, were scared to such a degree; that they threw away arms, ammunition and everything, and each man endeavored to shift for himself. The Indians followed about halfway to Fort Edward. The number killed on the road to Fort Edward is uncertain, as many were butchered in the woods and bushes, consequently, could not be all perceived by our people

who came away after. Near thirty carcasses, however, were actually seen, and from the frequent stenches they met, had reason to imagine, many more lay scattered about.

Finally, the blood bath ran its course. The Indians departed for Montreal with 400 prisoners, including Colonel Monro's Negro servant, their bloody trophies and loot. As they were leaving the fort site they came across 18 recent graves and, as a climax to their carnage, tore open the graves and scalped the bodies. The dead were all smallpox victims, one of them the brother of Robert Rogers of the Rangers.

As Kilby so aptly states it, "All the above treatment and confusion, proceeded from Montcalm's wilful neglect of sending a sufficient guard." Kilby's final comment is to the effect that it was as well that General Webb did not send reinforcements as they would have been sacrificed as well.

There is no question but what the French wanted to be at Fort William Henry, indeed had sustained hopes of taking Fort Edward and Albany as well, thereby effectively diminishing the British holdings in North America. The French had lost Fort Duquesne, but had soundly beaten the British at Oswego and literally obliterated a multitude of smaller British outposts in and near the Ohio Valley area.

This particular battle was different, possibly due to its locus being so close to Montreal, possibly the time of year. Whatever the reason, it had the earmarks of a Roman circus. Montcalm was the field commander; Lévis his number two, but the train contained as well Rigaud de Vaudreuil, who came, saw and lost in March (his position was that of governor of Three Rivers); Monsieur de Bourlamaque, Colonel of the Armies; and Chevalier de Montreuil, Major General – a rather awesome array of power figures.

One of Montcalm's aides was a young lieutenant by the name of Bougainville. His journals have left some small detail of life with the Indian of North America. This journal was published as "Adventures in the Wilderness; The American Journals of Louis Antoine de Bougainville."

Bougainville recounted in his journals how when he delivered a message from Montcalm, that Colonel Monro "returned many thanks for the courtesy of our nation and protested his joy at having to do with so generous an enemy." Louis Antoine de Bougainville was born in 1729. In 1764 he established a colony on the Falklands, surrendering it to the Spanish in 1766. From 1767 to 1769 he made a trip around the world, visiting Tahiti, the Samoan Group, the New Hebrides, and rediscovered the Solomon Islands; the largest of which is named for him. He name was also given to the strait between Bougainville and the Choiseul Islands, a strait in the New Hebrides and the Bougainvillea vine. He wrote a two volume set, "Description d'un Voyage Autour de Monde" on the morality of man in his natural state. He died in 1811. Pertaining to the massacre, he wrote his mother, "Some who would call themselves Frenchmen took part in the massacre."

Fact indicates the French had good to excellent control over the regulars, reasonable to nominal control over the militia and slight to none over the *coureurs de bois* and Indians. Evidence indicates that the French by the time of the capitulation had lost complete control of the Indians and were, in fact, fearful of them, although they were considered allies. This might explain the massacre, but does not excuse it.

Chapter Eleven

TOO LATE FOR TOO MANY

One of the most complex problems with the history of this battle has been the casualty figures. This problem was created through two factors; first were varying figures by different sources and second, nobody really knows how many died on the road to Fort Edward.

The original figures this author arrived at were 300 killed during the siege, 550 killed during the massacre, between 400 and 530 taken prisoner by the French, and 400 taken prisoner by the Indians and delivered to Montreal. Of those taken to Montreal, all would be ransomed by the French populace, except one who was killed and cooked by the Indians and his companions forced to eat him or suffer the same fate. The total figures appeared to be 851 known dead, 929 known survivors and between 420 and 720 missing and unaccounted for. This was based on a population count inclusive of Fort William Henry and Camp William Henry of between 2,070 and 2,500.

From Colonel Monro's figures, we now know that there were 2,140 fighting men, at least another 100 women and an unknown number of children. This brings the population count to a figure in excess of 2,240, probably 2,300.

Kilby indicates that two militia officers and 15 privates were killed within the first twenty-four to forty-eight hours. He further states that only 80 were killed during the siege with 10 of those being in the fort proper. He also puts the missing figure at 250.

We know from other sources that 80 New Hampshire militia surrendered en mass and were instantly massacred by the Indians. All the women and children, with the exception of one unidentified woman and child, were killed. The sick and wounded in the fort hospital and in the camp were killed as well.

Return of the Killed, Wounded and Missing (Corps Report) dated 25 August 1757. This item is reproduced by permission of The Huntington Library, San Marino, California. Loudon Collection, LO4313.

The corps report of killed, wounded and missing signed by Colonel Monro in Albany on 25 August 1757 reflects that four officers and 40 men were killed and an estimated 40 wounded. Of the regulars, inclusive of the 35th, 60th, Royal Artillery and Rangers, there were 20 killed, 22 wounded and 121 missing. Colonel Monro readily admits his figures for the militia are pure estimate. No count for the women and children was ever given.

Based on the figures we have from Monro's reports and memos, it appears that there were 2,200 men, women and children at Fort William Henry as of 3 August 1757. By daylight on 11 August, the figures read as follows:

406	killed – 97 during the siege, 308 during the massacre and 1 prisoner
536	missing
929	prisoners
429	reached Fort Edward
2300	total

Colonel Monro's corps report of killed, wounded and missing, which was written 15 days after the battle on 25 August, indicates the following:

701	accounted for, including some 272 who straggled in after 11 August
406	dead
929	prisoners
264	missing
2300	total

Is this an accurate figure? I trust it is. Considering the time lag involved, I do not believe it can get much more refined.

As for the French, no accurate count was ever given. Kilby estimates they had 200 killed during the siege. That is most likely a low figure. As you will recall, the French artillery commander sent his compliments to the British artillery officer, commending him on his most excellent use of his artillery.

There has never been any count of the Indian casualties during the siege or the massacre.

During the time frame 1755 to 1759 an estimated 6,000 British, French, Canadian and Indians lost their lives; a high price to pay for an area 64 miles long by 9 miles wide. That works out to 105 dead for each of the 576 square miles involved. It was indeed too late for too many.

Chapter Twelve

AFTERMATH

Surprisingly, the aftermath of the battle was already in motion by 10 August 1757. Former Captain, now Major Israel Putnam, was ordered out of Fort Edward by General Webb, with what appears to have been an all-Rangers relief column. They arrived at Fort William Henry on the 11th to a scene that must have staggered even the most hardened veteran.

The last of the French were disappearing down the lake in the distance. The fort was still burning and smoldering and the Rangers found parts of skulls and bones scattered amongst butchered, half-eaten bodies. Some parts were still cooking in the cooking fires. They were able to identify over a hundred female bodies in the burning fort, which was covered by a low-lying suffocating smoke and stench.

Major Israel Putnam was born in 1718 in Salem, Massachusetts. He was a farmer by trade. He served during King George's War and was a different type of officer than his peers. Rogers was a brilliant tactician with a solid hatred of the Indian. Stark was quiet, cautious, and a strict disciplinarian. Putnam was carefree and loved a challenge. There was a barracks fire at Fort Edward and Putnam climbed to the roof of the building and kept putting water on the fire, even though the powder magazine was next to the building. He eventually put out the fire, but burned his hands and face so badly that it was a month before he was released from the hospital.

Shorty after getting out of the hospital he was challenged by a British officer to fight a duel. As the challenged party, Putnam had his choice of weapons. He proposed that they each sit on a powder keg and, after the fuses were lit, the one who sat the longest would be considered the bravest and the winner. Both sat on their respective kegs and, as the fuses got shorter, the British officer jumped and fled.

Putnam got off his keg, walked over and put out the fuse on the officer's keg and returned to sit on his until the fuse burned out. The kegs contained highly dangerous onions. Putnam was captured by the Hurons in 1758, along with 14 other Rangers. The others were immediately butchered and scalped. The Hurons knew who he was, and harbored a special grudge against him. They tied him to a tree and a fire was built around him. They then proceeded to throw tomahawks at or near him with one grazing his cheek. Lieutenant Marin, the French Ranger officer heard of what was happening and rescued Putnam from certain death. Putnam would in 1764 see duty in Detroit and during the Revolution see action at Bunker Hill, Long Island and Forts Montgomery and Clinton in the Hudson Highlands. He sustained a paralytic stroke in 1779 and died in 1790.

Lieutenant Colonels Monro and Young were both prisoners of the French at Ticonderoga, or Carillon as the French called it. Monro was released and he returned to Albany or Fort Edward under escort, arriving at Fort Edward on the 16th of August. This is somewhat substantiated by an entry in Colonel Montressor's journal, that 11 of the survivors had come in on that date. The statement is somewhat misleading in that he is not specific as to whether all the prisoners from Carillon were returned or not. Apparently, not all were until the French started returning all the prisoners inclusive of those in Montreal, late in 1757. Morning reports from the 35th Regiment of Foot reflect that some of their personnel were returned as late as November.

Lieutenant Colonel Young was apparently at Carillon only on a temporary basis, being removed for more extensive and much needed medical care. He was wounded once and conducted the capitulation talks with the French while wounded. There is some evidence that he also had a second wound. The worst was in his leg, and from his letters, it seems the bone may have been chipped.

John Young has been something of a mystery all these years. His letters from 1737 to 1761 are located in the Loudon collection at the Huntington Library in San Marino, California. He apparently was from the border country or Scotland proper. He appears to have been an intimate of Lord Loudon and quite possibly was his protégé. He was a lieutenant in 1737, a major in 1756, lieutenant colonel in 1757 and was a full colonel by 1761.

He saw service in London, New York, Philadelphia and on the frontier. He was the regular army officer commanding under Colonel John Stanwix of the Royal Americans. They are well-known as the 60th, but were originally founded as the 62nd. The numerical change occurred for whatever reason within the first six months from the time the unit was formed. It was primarily composed of men from Pennsylvania. The three battalions of this unit served in South Carolina, New York and apparently in the general Philadelphia area. Several recruits came from New Jersey.

John Young was married and his wife lived in New York. He was something of a socialite as he knew Generals Abercrombie and Amherst, Lord Hair, Lord Porine, Lord Primrose, Lord Home, Lord Sinclair, Lady Mary Cunningham, Glen Eagles, and Sandy Baird on a personal basis and was well-versed in the facts of the Young Pretender's Invasion from Holland. He also knew the rather infamous Captain Monk. The captain surrendered a Scottish position without a shot to 20 French unarmed pioneers. His letters to Loudon indicate that Loudon may well have been married to his sister.

Lieutenant Colonel Young wrote three letters during the siege; one appears to be a statement concerning troop strength, another appears to be to General Webb and a third, a document supporting Colonel Monro's decision on capitulation.

Camp Near Fort Wm. Henry
Augs 4th 1757

When General Webb detached me from Fort Edward, I had no written instructions, but as I have a copy of inquiries in which the garrison of Fort Edward is fixed at 100 Regulars and 200 irregulars, and as I think the general says an equal number was sufficient for Fort Wm Henry while the communication to the fort was open, therefor I have given it as my opinion that while we have it in our power to throw what troops we please into that fort, the present garrison of about 330 men is full sufficient for the present duty.

John Young LtCol
Royal American Regt.

Dear Sir
To my legg is in a fair way of doing well, yet it does not recover so fast as I first expected, as soon as I am able to under take the journey, I shal certainly vett out from this.

I question very much if My Lord Loudon will come up country, the accounts he will then receive will be so very contrary to his expectations that I am apt to believe he will stop short, in which case/begging pardon for advising you/I should think it very proper for you to pay his Lordship a visit at York, and lay before him a duplicate of all the letters you wrote and received and also a full narration of the whole transaction, as in all probability the dispatches you have already sent to His Lordship have miscarried; writing a bed is not quite easy to me as you may see by this so shal only add that I am with the greatist sincerity and esteem

My Dear Sir
Your Most Faithful Friend
and Most Affect. Obedient
Humble Servant
John Young

Fort Edward
August 8th 1757

Camp near Fort William Henry Tuesday 9th August 1757

Upon a representation to George Monro Surg Lieut. Colonel of His Majesty's 35th Regiment of Foot and commanding all the Forces at Lake George, by several officers Commanding Corps in this camp that they were of opinion nothing further could be done for the defense of Fort Wm. Henry, they therefore desired that a council of war should be called, which was accordingly composed of the following officers: Who were unanimously of opinion that considering the barriers that have been erected and the near approaches the enemy has lately made, which are ready to play within one hundred yards of the Fort and likewise the excessive bad conditions of the remaining artillery, the greatest part of the largest and most serviceable pieces being already burst, and that all communication between we and Fort Edward being cut off ever since the 3th instant, as appears by a letter from Major General Webb, dated at Fort Edward the 4th instant, the only intelligence we have now been able to come at and confirming also from the whole tenor of the above mentioned letter a copy of which here unto annexed/that there was not the slight expectation either of relief or saucor from General Webb, without which it was impossible to continue the defense of the Fort and Camp Longer, than has already been done; They therefore have requested Lieu. Colonel Monro/whose behavior upon this occasion they are all thoroughly satisfied with and take this public opportunity to return him their thanks for the same/to send a deputation to the French General Mons. Montcalm to obtain honourable terms for the troops in the camp and garrison in the fort. Upon deliveriing it up into his hand....

Given under our hands at the camp near Fort Wm.
Henry this 9th day of August 1757.

> John Young LtCol
> Chas. Ince Capt. 35th
> Luke Gardiner Capt. 35th
> Wm. Bamford Lt. 35th
> Will Hamilton Lt. 35th
> R. Taesch Royal Artillery
> Chas. Chruckshanks Capt
> Indep Comp
> Joseph Frye Col Mass Rgt
> John Parker Col Jersey Rgt
> John Gosse (Goffe)
> Col New Hampshire Rgt
> John Gilman Maj of New Hamp
> Richard Saltonstall
> Capt Mass Rgt
> Jonathan Ogden Capt of Rangers

In a letter dated 20 September 1757, Colonel Young wrote to Lord Loudon of still having problems with small pieces of bone. By 1761 he was a full colonel. John Stanwix had been promoted to general and was to have a fort at the present day site of Rome, New York named for him.

According to the letter signed by the officers at Fort William Henry, they had nothing left with which to fight a defense. In Kilby's narrative he indicated that the French actually captured 1,800 barrels of pork; 1,400 barrels of flour and other species of provisions not in proportionate amounts. They also captured one 12-round cannon, two 9-pounders, and four 4-pounders as well as one 7-inch howitzer; a very few shells and a very little musket ball and powder.

This coincides with what it is alleged Colonel Monro reported as captured and what the commandant of Fort Carillon is also alleged to have inventoried.

Montcalm's list reads as if he captured the entire munitions and defensive system of the fort. What follows is his list and, if what are believed to be other reliable sources, are correct, it is a masterpiece of either wishful thinking or out-and-out padding of the books.

17	pieces of cannon, from 32 to 5 pounds, of which two brass and three are unfit for service
2	9-inch mortars, burst during the siege
1	9-inch howitzer
1	6-inch iron mortar
13	small iron swivels
1	shot grating
227	barrels of powder at 100 pounds each
227	barrels of powder at 50 pounds each
2,308	pieces of shot of diverse calibre
360	6 and 9-inch shell
185	12-inch shell
4	cases of balls of 200 pounds each
1	case of grenades
6	cases of fireworks
6	brass guns, 2 of 12 pounds and 4 of 15 pounds.
4	iron swivels
215	shot
75	barrels of powder at 25 pounds each
80	gun charges in caissons
600	pounds of ball
50	pounds of match
23	cannon, 8 are brass
1	fire howitzer
1	mortar
17	swivels
35,835	pounds of powder
2,522	shot
1,400	pounds of ball
1	grenade chest
6	chests of fireworks, grapeshot of diverse calibre
3,000	barrels of flour or pork

Colonel Monro provided Lord Loudon with as much information concerning the siege as was possible. His letters and memos follow in the order of calendar date.

Albany 20 August 1757

My Lord
I have the honor to send your Lordship, all the letters, and papers, relative to, Fort Wm. Henry, from the morning it was invested, which was the 3rd inst. To the day, the capitulation was sign'd, which was the 9th Inst. 12 o'clock at noon. I am with greatest respect.
Your Lordships
Most faithful and
very obd. Humble Servant
Geo Monro
LtCol. 35 Regmt.

Gen. Webbs letter dated 3rd August, I received the evening of that day.

His letter dated 4th August, I received the 6th, by Gen Montcalms aid de camp.

His letter dated 6th August, was given to me, by a Ranger between 8 and 9 o'clock of the 9th August at night the day the capitulation was signed.

His letter dated the 8th August was sent to me, by Gen. Montcalm about 6 o'clock in the evening, the 9th August after the capitulation.

N.B. Those were all the letters, I received during the time of the siege.

Albany 30th August 1757

My Lord
I did myself the honor to send your Lordship, the 18th Inst. Directed to Halifax, a copy of the

capitulation, signed by M. Montcalm the French Gen. And me; at Fort Wm. Henry the 9th inst. And likeways the letters, that past between Gen. Webb and me, from the 3rd of August, which was the day they invested the place, to the 9th, 12 o'clock, at noon, which was the time, the capitulation was signed. The capitulation was broke, by plundering, both the officers and soldiers, M. Montcalm has wrote your Lordship, a letter telling how much he regretted the usage we met with, and that it was not in his power to prevent it, and how he had greatly expos'd his person to danger, to prevent it, that particular fact never came to my knowledge, though I went after this happen'd, to his camp, where I remained from the Wednesday at noon, till Monday morning following, he likeways tells your Lordship that what happen'd was in some measure owing to the liquor, the Indians got in our camp, which is really not fact as I myself saw every drop of liquor distroy'd immediately after the capitulation was sign'd. I have the honor to be.

Your Lordships
Most faithful and very
Obedient Humble Servant
Geo. Monro
Lt.Col 35 Regmt

The letter from General Montcalm containing the allegations that the Indians were able to gain control of and drink the liquor in the British camp, that Colonel Monro refers to were forwarded by the town priest of De La Rechelle, North America to Monsieur le Count d'Affrey for publication in the Dutch newspapers. He also forwarded a copy of the letter from Vaudreuil to Loudon regarding the precautions for guarding the English garrison of the Fort William Henry from the cruelties of the savages. Included is part of the letter of the priest.

All of the accounts which were received here about the capture of the Fort George or William Henry by

Canada made mention of the violence that the English garrison suffered on the part of the savages. But those who concur, all have said that the dispatchment of these precautions that Monsieur de Montcalm had taken, it can be guaranteed that they were conducted in a tranquil manner to Fort Edward. If the soldiers did not have the imprudence of distribution to the savages the intoxicating liquors, that Monsieur de Montcalm and he principal French officers did unhesitatingly expose themselves completely with great danger in order to calm the savages and that Monsieur de Vaudreuil was obliged to use all of his authority to return them into the hands of the English who were most grateful. One finds in authentic detail everything that happened on this occasion in these two letters written to Monsieur le Count of Loudon, the first by Monsieur de Montcalm and the second by Monsieur de Vaudreuil.

Thus was the setup for a written political coverup of a major loss of command and control. Montcalm's letter is first and Vaudreuil's is second.

My Lord
   The honorable defence of the Lieutenant Colonel Monroe was determined by me to have accorded to him and his garrison an honorable surrender. It has not suffered the least alteration. If your soldiers had not given you rumor that the troops had wanted to leave with more order and not to have suffered the terror of our savages who have become emboldened in these last days; to them a word. France had wanted to force the completion of this that I have secured for her proper advantage. The attention paid to them was like bad luck for them, as I had with me the Abenakis of Panaonaniski in Acadia who thought to their pity that they had received some bad treatment from the English. You know that this was a contingent of 300 savages from 33 different nations; and I fear lest the

Commander of the fort would condem me. I consider myself lucky that the disorder was not as troublesome to them as I might have feared that it could have been. The army knows that I was personally exposed at the same time that my officers defending them were rendering justice to all that I had put in this cause. Also My Lord, I pray to you to fulfill the surrender in all areas, the least nonfulfillment on the slightest pretext will be of one more vexatious consequence for you which makes one more for me. I have taken from the savages more than 400 prisoners and they will be assembled by the Monsieur de Vaudreuil, to whom I have dispatched a courier and they will be brought by an army battalion in a packet-boat for their most secure safety to Louisbourg. The commander of this place, picked by me rather than Halifax. At the time of the orthodox reassembly for the surrender the few French and Canadian that you have been able to have as prisoners since the beginning of this war, I report on the number to your Lordship. It beseeches me namely due to the Canadian force who were sent back by the surrender, by the strength of the necessity. I ask you to see to it to drive to Halifax in order to be exchanged with them, those of yours that I have sent back to Louisbourg.

    I had to take great care of the new Captain (Rudolphus Faesch – Royal Americans) that has stayed as a guarantee of the surrender and the wounded Captain (Ormsby – 35th) that I have already brought to Montreal with a surgeon, who will receive all the assistance possible. I join to this letter one that I have the honor to write to you for the sake of the Lieutenant Colonel Young, and which will prove to you the high esteem that I have for Your Excellency.

Am, Sieur?

My Lord
    Monsieur de Montcalm has rendered me an account of the letter that he has written Your

Excellency on the 14th of the past month as to the responsibility of General Webb in order to instruct him of all that concerns the surrender that he settled the 9th of the same month in force of the power that I had given to him, to the garrison of the Fort William Henry, and to the troops that were in the fortified joint camp.

I have nothing to add to this that he has written to Your Excellency about what has happened on behalf of the savages. It is very unfortunate, My lord, that these troops of his British Majesty were themselves, in some instances, persisting to want to make premature the time for their departure and that some English soldiers had the imprudence to give to savages some alcoholic drinks in spite of the express recommendations in response to this.

Colonel Monro, his staff and generally, all the officers of the garrison and of the fortified camp who had been given good and safe escort to Edward did not have the right to have allowed Your Excellency to not know that Monsieur Le Marquis de Montcalm, and the principal French officers had exposed their own selves for the whole night to keep the English from emancipating concealed savages. These Monsieurs, My Lord, were each one consistent with the generosity that I have constantly exercised in respect to the English prisoners that I had repurchased from the savages the year before and the preceding years. Your Excellency had not the power to have knowledge of those whom I sent back the previous autumn. Monsieur the new Royal American Captain who has been given to him as hostage for the ordinance of the surrender was a witness of the pains that I have taken upon myself in order to prevent the course of the ferocity of the Indian nations, and in order to bind the hands of the English from the surrender of Fort William Henry and all of the same ones of the garrison of that fort who were violently captured by the savages sometime before the surrender in the battle, or the detachment that Colonel Parker had led. I have attempted to dress and treat well all these prisoners. I did not have to be stopped that time for the considerable sum that it had cost him – The King, for these repurchases nor from the defenseless who were inseparable. I do not forget for an instant to bring back Your Excellency, to Halifax from the diverse parliamentarians, Monsieur Faesch and the English from the garrison and from the entrenchment of the Fort William Henry. They have all asked me to take that route, for them the most safe, that of the Lac St. Sacrement would be very risky on account of the savages. I am satisfied by the return of the first ordinance of the surrender. In respect to the other English of whom I have the honor to speak to you about, that I also redeemed from the savages who absolutely wanted to keep them in their power, who waited because they had no one to tell them of the surrender, they stayed near me like prisoners of war. I am very flattered to have this occasion in order to give to Your Excellency and account of the evidence of the humanity and of the generosity that the French nation made at all times, which I believe is a testimony of the justice that the French nation has rendered in this regard. I direct to the Commander of Halifax the English roster that I sent back to Your Excellency and he will, in turn give it to him.

 I hope that you would like to take possession of these persons from the ordinary right accorded to the parliamentarians, who have acquired the right. The testimonies of Monsieur Faesch are very sufficient to me to justify to Your Excellency and to all of Europe that what I have done makes clear how delicate the independence and caprice of the Indian nations are, which is well known. All this I owe in accordance to rules of war and to the tendency that the French have naturally to relieve the unfortunate. These sentiments, My Lord, I have promoted in favor of the English, the proof that I have given to them and that I reiterate with pleasure to Your Excellency. They are to me a sure guarantee of his exactitude and of his punctuality to complete Ordinance 5 of the surrender and that is relative to the item which I have the honor of beseeching you My Lord, that of very much wanting to bring back before the expiration of the set date of this article, in good care to Carillon, the French prisoners, Canadians and savages of all sex, who are in the Provinces of New England since the beginning of the war or the hostilities in America. The Northerners, particularly Monsieur le Baron de Longueil, has given me news, that the Sieurs Lacros and Gaucher, militia officers and others had been violently captured on the 8 September 1755 in the matter of Monsieur Le Baron Diskeau. It is no longer in my power about the wounded or sick English who are here on the list, that I have deferred to Monsieur Faesch. I will keep them until the exchange is completed and then I will bring them back to Your Excellency in accordance with Article 7 of the surrender. I intend to take very good care of them. Monsieur Harbe, the Captain, is doing much better and I hope that his leg can be saved. I will continue to look for more solid resources in order to bear this war in the least cruel manner possible. In this Your Excellency is completely in agreeance to avail himself with permission of the Indian nations. I neglect nothing in my attempt to put a curb on their ferocity. I do not doubt that Your Exellency does not think or act likewise, but I will have the honor of informing him that if our prisoners are not recovered immediately there will be in lieu of freedom, fear that the savages who desire them will carry them to the farthest extremities away from the English.

  I approve of the letter that Monsieur Le Marquis de Montcalm has written to Your Excellency for the sake of the Lieutenant Colonel Young in order that he "toe the mark", not obstinately surrender, in order to exercise the direction of the Governor of Virginia. I may but barely get to know him since I will myself be

"toeing the mark." I will always be charmed to personally give to Your Excellency tokens of consideration that I have for him and the respectful sentiments who those to whom I have the honor to be Sieur Vaudreuil.
Governor

Both letters, although diplomatic in scope and content, are really an attempted coverup of the massacre and more obviously thinly veiled threats of what will happen to the British prisoners if the terms of the capitulation are not met. As to whether the Indians were under the influence, it is something of a moot point. One source has indicated fully half of them were. Kilby makes no mention of it and no factual sources indicating they were have been found. It is possible that this allegation was used to offset what happened in the mind of Montcalm. It is of note that he indicates he had some 3,000 Indians with him. One French prisoner indicated 4,500 and Kilby states 1,500 Indians. Evidence tends to indicate at least the 3,000 claimed by Montcalm.

The Indians had many young men who had never tasted what they referred to as "The Brew." This was, in fact, human blood, which could be counted as human heads or scalps in some tribes and in others the actual drinking of fresh human blood and eating of human flesh.

As the dust slowly settled after the massacre, Lieutenant Colonel Monro petitioned the Earl of Loudon for assignment as a battalion commander with the Royal Americans. He referred to his 36 years of continuous service and the fact that he never had the honor to receive a commission that he did not purchase. There is no question but that he was turned down, as his next petition, which is attached as an exhibit, revealed a secret that was unknown for over 200 years – even to the Monro clan of Scotland. That petition also revealed why there was an obvious distance between him and the corps and general staff. That petition reads as follows:

> To the Kings Most Excellent Majesty
> The Petition of George Monro Surgeon
> Your petitioner humbly begs leave to represent to your Majesty that he has now served in the services in quality of a surgeon for the space of twenty years, by far the best of his life, during which period he has bore a considerable part in the service during the last war in Flanders and Scotland and during almost all the present war in North America, and West India where tho he has had only the appointment of a surgeon to the hospital, he has constantly performed the duty of a Physican, almost the last two years he has had a commission from General Amherst to act as Assistant Physician to the hospital at Martinico and since his return to North America with the sick has constantly acted in the same capacity.
> After the last of his days spent in this manner, your petitioner finds that he has no prospect from his present situation of any better provision for the remainder of his life than the small allowance of five shillings a day half pay when his service is no more wanted.
> And at the same time finds that during the course of the present war many who entered upon their dutys some years after he had been in the service, particularly almost all the Senior Surgeons have been preferred so as to entitle them to a better half pay than five shillings a day.
> Your petitioner therefore humbly prays Your Majesty that you will be pleased to take his case into consideration and put him upon the half pay of a Physician.

The petition is unsigned.

The morning report of the 35th Rgt of Foot dated 20 November 1757 reflects that Lieutenant Colonel Monro died 3 November 1757 at Albany. The strain had been too much on Colonel Monro and his health failed. He died of a heart attack at the age of 57 on the streets of Albany on 3rd November 1757. He was buried the following day at St. Peter's Episcopal Church, Albany, New York.

Colonel George Monro was a man of mystery for over 200 years. His name was the only thing that was known of him. He was the son of Colonel George Monro and Margaret Bruce, born about 1700 in Clonfin, County Longford, Ireland. He was the youngest son, having an older brother, Alexander, and a younger sister, Margaret. His father was one of the original captains of the Cameronians – 26th Foot, and saw active and honourable service at the Battle of Dunkeld in 1689. He also served with an independent company of Foot at Perthshire and served as a Major in Sir Charles Graham's Foot in the siege of Namur in 1695. He was promoted to Colonel in 1716.

Young George came from a solid military background. He entered the service in Otway's Regiment, later the 35th Foot, later the Royal Sussex and now part of the Queen's Regt. His career can be followed by his promotions; Lieutenant, 9th August 1718; Captain, 27th September 1727; Major, 18th August 1747; and Lieutenant Colonel, 4th January 1750.

It was believed until his petition for retirement was found that Fort William Henry was the Colonel's first major action. He handled it in an exemplary manner, particularly in view of the fact that he fought until there was nothing left to fight with and then sought relief for his troops, the women and children through the only avenue left him. This the officers under him attested to in writing, as did General Montcalm.

Military decorations were few and far between in the 1700s. Usually the officer received a grant to the Peerage. Later there would be the Victoria Cross, Military Cross and George Medal. Colonel Monro would receive none of these. In January 1758 he was gazetted a full colonel.

By the terms of his will Colonel Monro did not want the location of his grave known. So it remained, until the clansman, Keith Monroe of Miskayuna, New York located it. On 4th November 1984, a memorial service was held at

St. Peter's Church. A memorial plaque was placed in the church in early 1985. Colonel Monro has a headstone.

By the terms of his will, dated 7th February 1756, his sons George and Sackville and daughter Jane were to receive equal shares of his estate along with a nephew John, whom I believe was the third Laird of Auchinbowie in Scotland. This will was probated on 17th November 1759 in Prerogative Court. No mention is made of the children's mother and indeed the children are referred to as either refuted or reputed. The correct spelling of the name is Monro, although Munro and Monroe are also used and accepted.

The 35th Regiment was originally raised in Belfast in 1701 by the 3rd Earl of Donegal at his own expense. King William III gave permission for the regiment to wear orange facings as a special mark of his favor. The regiment was first known as "The Belfast Regiment." Commonly, in the army it was referred to as the "Orange(s)." Later it was called the "Otways Regiment." At the same time it had the designation "35th Regiment of Foot," later the "Royal Sussex" and until recently a battalion was part of the "Queen's Regiment." Under the recent amalgamation in the army it is no more. The regiment first saw duty as a rapid deployment force aboard navy ships during the Wars of Spanish Succession from 1704 to 1707.

It arrived in Nova Scotia in 1756 and served on the line at Louisbourg until March of 1757 when ordered to Fort William Henry.

The maps indicating the line of battle during the Siege of Louisbourg under General Amherst in 1758, show the 35th Foot to be at the center of the line. No greater honor could have been given this regiment. During the Battle of Quebec in 1759, the regiment, again at the center of the line, exacted partial revenge for Fort William Henry. They found themselves facing the Royal Roussillons, one of the units that had stood by while the Hurons indulged in their blood bath at the fort. The 35th defeated the Roussillons. After the battle they picked up the white cockades the French wore on their hats. The cockade has since been incorporated in the badge of the regiment as a white plume and is still present in the badge of the Queen's Regiment. In 1960, the Royal Sussex raised a memorial cairn at the site of the battle on Lake George.

That plaque reads as follows:

This plaque commemorates the memory of those officers, N.C.O.s and men of the 35th Regiment of Foot (now The Royal Sussex Regiment), their wives and families, who lost their lives during the defense of Fort William Henry, and the subsequent massacre by hostile Red Indians after the surrender and evacuation of the Fort in 1757. The Royal Sussex Regimental Association, Roussillon Barracks, Chichester, Sussex.

Two final things came out of the aftermath of the massacre: thousands of Indians would die as a result of the scalping of the smallpox victims' bodies (a bitter answer to the tasting of "The Brew"); and the British finally came to realize they had a long, hard battle ahead of them to gain control of North America.

First Battalion of the 62d or Royal American Regiment.

Ranks.	Names.	Observations.
Colonel	John Stanwix	
~~Colonel~~	~~Peter Williams~~	
Captain Lieut.	John Dalrymple	Colonel's Company
Lieutenant	George Turnbull	Ca Capt. ~~Rutherford~~ James Campbell
Ensign	Brereton Saynton	
Lieu. Colonel	Henry Bouquet	
~~Captain~~	~~Hicson~~	
Lieutenants	Gilbert III. Oslan	1st Col. Comp.º — Sentrieck
	Brown	Hollandt Dec.
Ensign	Thomas Campbell	
Major	John Young	
Lieut.	Charles Forbes	
	Mackay	Maj. Comp.
Ensign	William Ridge	Barnsley
Captain	John Tullikens	
Lieut.	Donald Campbell	4 Comp.
	Hefser	
Ensign	Stair Campbell Carr.	
Captain	Munster	
Lieut.	George Warburton	5. Comp.
	Brehm	
Ensign	Watson	
Captain	Ralph Harding	
Lieut.	Robert Drew	6. Comp.
	Kleinbull	
Ensign	William Ryder	
Captain	Richard Mather	
Lieut.	Allan	7. Comp.
	Van Ingen	
Ensign	Townsend Guy	
Captain	Francis Lander	
Lieut.	Mayer	8. Comp.
Ensign	Edward Jenkins	
Captain	Gavin Cochran	
Lieut.	John Jacky	9. Comp. Gil. McAdam
	John Lealy	
Ensign	Francis Mackay	
Captain	Alex. Harlord	Stanwix
Lieut.	George Fullerton	10. Comp.
Ensign		

Roster of Officers of the 1st Battalion of the 62nd Regiment of Foot or Royal Americans (Later known as the 60th Royal Americans). This item is reproduced by permission of *The Huntington Library, San Marino, California.* Loudon Collection, LO6953.

Roster of Officers of the Royal Americans. This item is reproduced by permission of *The Huntington Library, San Marino, California.* Loudon Collection, LO6952.

Monthly Returns dated 25 November 1757 and 25 December 1757 (p. 121), both with notations of Col. Monro's death. These items are reproduced by permission of *The Huntington Library, San Marino, California.* Loudon Collection, LO6751.

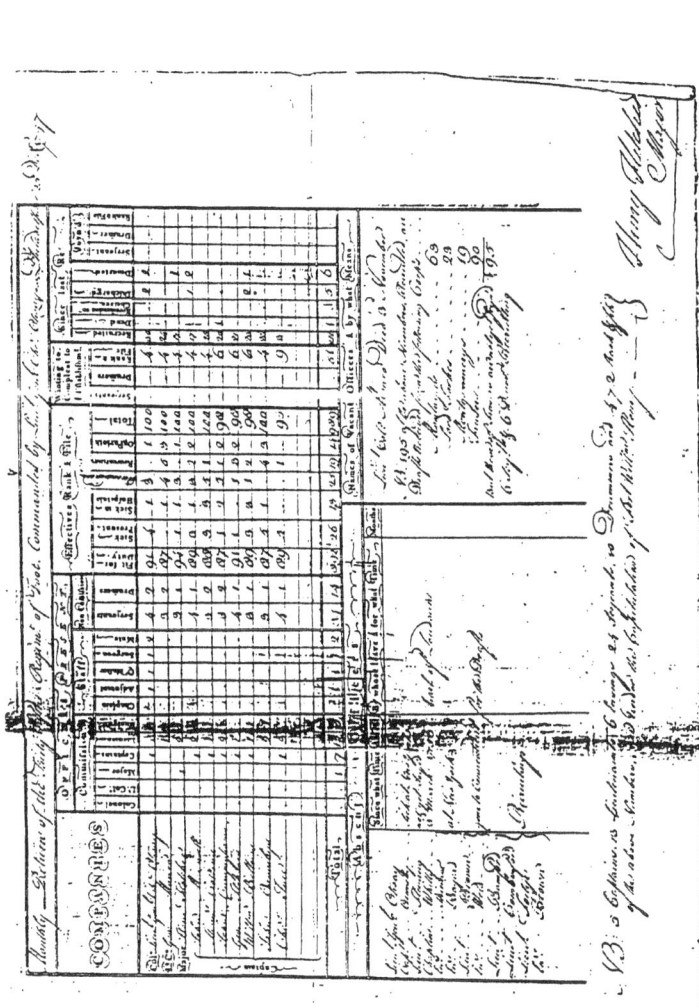

Monthly Returns dated 25 December 1757 and 25 November 1757 (p. 120), both with notations of Col. Monro's death. These items are reproduced by permission of *The Huntington Library, San Marino, California*. Loudon Collection, LO6751.

To The Kings Most Excellent Majesty

The Petition of George Monro Surgeon.

Your Petitioner humbly begs leave to represent to your Majesty that he has now Served in the Service in quality of a Surgeon for the Space of Twenty Years; by far the best of his life; during which period he has bore a Considerable part in the Service during the last War in Flanders and Scotland and during almost all the present war in North America, and West Indies where tho' he has had only the appointment of a Surgeon to the Hospital he has constantly performed the duty of a Physician. Almost the last two years he has had a Commission from General Amherst to act as Assistant Physician to the Hospital at Martinico and since his return to North America with the Sick, has constantly acted in the same Capacity.

After the best of his days Spent in this manner Your Petitioner finds that he has no prospect from his present situation of any better Provision for the remainder of his life than the Small allowance of Five Shillings a day half pay when his Service is no more wanted.

And at the same time finds that during the course of the present War many who entered upon their duty some Years after he had been in the Service, particularly almost all the Senior Surgeons have been preferred, so as to intitle them to a better Half pay than five Shillings a day.

Your

Your Petitioner therefore Humbly prays your Majesty that you will be pleased to take his case into Consideration and put him upon the Half pay of a Physician.

Pages 122-123: Lt. Col. Monro's petition for retirement as a physician. This item is reproduced by permission of *The Huntington Library, San Marino, California.* Loudon Collection, LO5994.

Chapter Thirteen

FINAL CHAPTER

The war continued. In July 1758, General James Abercromby, known as "Mrs. Nabby Crombie" to his men, assaulted Carillon without taking it. This fiasco ruined him and encouraged the French. If he had listened to Ranger Captain Stark he would have won. He sent his chief engineer and Stark forward to survey the fort. His engineer reported, "Their works are flimsy." Stark advised that this was not the case. Abercromby felt Stark was a bumpkin and refused to listen. As a result, he lost over 2,000 men while Montcalm, who was in charge at Carillon, lost some 400. The Black Watch Regiment, 42nd Foot, was almost decimated in repeated assaults against the French defenses.

Little is known about General James Abercromby. (That is the correct spelling, although the "ie" ending is more commonly seen.) He was born in Scotland in 1706 and was a soldier by profession. He arrived in the colonies in 1756 and in 1758 replaced Lord Loudon as Supreme Commander. After his failure at Carillon he was removed from position and replaced by General Jeffrey Amherst. He then became attorney general for the Carolina Plantations. He died in 1781.

On the way to Carillon, Captain Stark had as a tent mate, Viscount, Brigadier George Augustus, Lord Howe. Lord Howe was the darling of the regulars. He insisted that all men in his command, including himself, undergo training with the Rangers. He was charming, efficient, a gentleman and always fair with his troops. On the march he carried his own blanket and bearskin, did his own washing, ate out of a communal bowl with a clasp knife and handled his own weapons. He was the youngest of three brothers; the oldest, the Earl, Admiral Richard Howe; and Viscount, the General William Howe. His two brothers would become famous during the Revolution and would eventually become known as strong supporters of the colonies, all outward appearances to the contrary.

During a patrol action prior to the attempt on Carillon, French were encountered and shots exchanged. A French bullet entered Howe's heart, killing him instantly and with him much of the enthusiasm of the British army. He was buried next to Colonel Monro at St. Peter's Church in Albany.

Shortly after the fiasco at Carillon, a supply train was ambushed near Glens Falls, New York by a composite force of some 400 French and Indians under the command of a Canadian known simply as La Corne. The train consisted of 30 wagons pulled by 60 oxen, plus another 60 oxen, 100 soldiers, 50 teamsters and 12 women. There were also about 130 oxen being driven in herd for use as beef. The train was totally destroyed with two oxen being left alive. They would later be killed by the patrol that found the disaster as one had been scalped and the other had a horn gouged out.

La Corne was born in the fall of 1711. He was an officer in the colonial regular troops, a merchant, interpreter and member of the Legislative Council. He was also the second largest slave owner in Canada. The French used Indians, mainly Pawnees from the Mississippi area, as slaves. He served in King George's War and was at the fall of Fort Clinton with Joseph Marin and Rigaud Vaudreuil. He was at Fort William Henry in command of the troops and Indians blocking the military road and was designated one of the officers of the escort to take the British to Fort Edward. French records indicate that in the ambush against the supply train he took 64 prisoners and 80 scalps. Governor-General Vaudreuil decorated him for his action.

After the war he decided to go to France. He sailed on 15th October 1761. The ship he was on sank a month later near Cape North on Cape Breton Island. He survived and after a trip of 550 leagues arrived in Quebec on 23rd February 1762. The trip took him 100 days.

He stayed on in Canada and two of his daughters married into British families; one married John Campbell and the other Major John Lennox. He was in charge of Burgoyne's

Hyenas, as his Indian allies were referred to by Edmund Burke in a speech to Parliament. He is also alleged to have been instrumental in Pontiac's uprising in 1763. Burgoyne would blame La Corne for the desertion of his Indians at the Battle of Saratoga. However, Burgoyne was at fault as the Indians had been disgusted by Burgoyne's indifference and callousness toward their dead and wounded after the Battle of Bennington.

He became a member of the Legislative Council in 1765 and a councillor in 1769. Even with these prestigious positions the Americans and British would never completely trust him, most considering him to be, in the words of Governor Guy Carleton of Canada, "a great villain and as cunning as the devil." He died 1 October 1784 at his home in Montreal and was buried in the chapel of Sainte-Anne in the church of Notre-Dame.

General Amherst arrived in the colonies in early 1758 as a major general to command the Louisbourg campaign. After taking Louisbourg in the summer of 1758 he relieved Abercromby as supreme commander. In the summer of 1759 he took Fort Carillon and proceeded to Crown Point (or Fort St. Frederic) only to find it deserted and a smoldering ruin. In September 1759, Quebec fell, with it came the deaths of Generals James Wolfe and Montcalm.

Francis Parkman, among others, did yeoman service to General Wolfe in his book, *Montcalm and Wolfe*, but one remark should be made about Wolfe. In a letter to a friend in England he described northern New York and Canada as the most horrid lands, having only two seasons; June, July, August and winter.

General Jeffery Amherst, Baron Amherst, was born in 1717. His whole life was spent in the army. He served in the War of the Austrian Succession and in the early part of the Seven Years' War. He came to the colonies in 1758. He took Louisbourg, Carillon and Crown Point and in 1760 directed the capture of Montreal. He is also credited rightly or wrongly with having invented germ warfare. He is alleged to have purposely infected trade blankets with smallpox germs before giving them to the Indians. He returned to England in 1763.

During the War of Independence he refused to serve in the colonies against the colonials. In 1778 he was promoted to commander in chief of home defenses. He was created a baron in 1776 and promoted to field marshal in 1796. He died in 1797. Amherst College in Massachusetts is named after him.

In the fall of 1759 Robert Rogers and some 200 Rangers attacked the Abenaki village at St. Francis. Rogers found over 600 scalps waving from poles in the morning breeze. Rogers killed most of the inhabitants, fired the village and left as there was a strong force of French and Indians nearby. Rogers brought out with him what white prisoners there were. He would lose approximately two-thirds of his force on the return trip to ambushes and starvation.

In April 1758, Brigadier General John Forbes, Colonel Commanding – 17th Foot, assembled a force of 1,600 men composed of Montgomery's Highlanders, a battalion of the 60th Foot, provincials from Virginia and some southern Indians. They came together in Philadelphia to march against Fort Duquesne.

By November, as Forbes command came within short miles of Fort Duquesne, Major James Grant requested permission to take a force of 800 Highlanders and Virginians to attack and try to carry Fort Duquesne. The force apparently became lost in the dark and were attacked by the French and their Indian allies. Some 100, including Major Grant, were killed.

He and his Highlanders were saluted for their bravery and fighting skills by the Indians. Forbes' command found a circle of oak stakes on which the heads of Grant and the Highlanders were impaled with their kilts wrapped around the stakes. The Indians considered them strong as oak, brave and courageous fighters.

As Forbes proceeded to within a mile of the fort, the French blew it up and fled. Forbes left a small detachment, renaming it "Pittsborough" or "Pitt"; returning to

Philadelphia on a litter as he was dying from dysentery. He died a hero shortly after his return to Philadelphia.

On 25 August 1758, Lieutenant Colonel John Bradstreet attacked the French Fort Frontenac on Lake Ontario. With its capture and destruction, French control of Lake Ontario was lost.

One month earlier to the day, Fort Niagara was captured from the French by Sir William Johnson. All that was left to the French was Detroit and Michillimackinac. In three years, the fortunes of war had come 180 degrees. The year 1760 would see the fall of Quebec and Montreal. Wolfe and Montcalm would both die at Quebec and with them the heart went out of the French and English both.

The Peace Treaty was signed at Ghent in 1763 and with its signing, Canada became British.

Chapter Fourteen

POSTSCRIPT

This book dealt with the battle of Fort William Henry. Other writers, such as Francis Parkman and E. P. Hamilton, have written about the whole French and Indian War. John R. Cuneo wrote about Robert Rogers in great detail. Kenneth Roberts wrote about Rogers' raid on St. Francis and a multitude of writers have written about the various Indian wars, French and British expansion in North America.

It has taken 20 years of research to compile this book. The burning question in the author's mind – is it accurate? I believe it is. I'm sure there are hundred of documents lying around in archives or someone's attic that could provide more information. Finding them is the problem.

Although I have drawn a few conclusions in writing, I have tried to present a battle as it was seen through the eyes of the people who were there. I'm sure that other individuals see it in a different light.

On my first visit to Fort William Henry, some of the remains of those who fought and died there were visible. On Memorial Day, 1993, a memorial service was held for the dead of the fort and a memorial grave site dedicated. The remains are all buried now and hopefully, the souls of the individuals who died there are at rest.

In reviewing the manuscript, I note that I left some items out. It was pure error, but errors happen. Ranger Carver did have a first name. He has been referred to as both James and Jonathan and the latter appears to be the correct name. Robert Rogers was proscribed by the New Hampshire Assembly in 1778. According to the bill passed by the Assembly, he, or any other British sympathizer would be returned to the British if caught in New Hampshire. The second time they were caught, they would be killed. Feelings ran high and sometimes just a bit too high.

At one point I felt that the area involved in the battle of Fort William Henry, which extends from Fort Edward on the south to Crown Point on the north, should be referred to as "The Up-Down, Wet-dry, Elongated Battleground." I still feel it is an apt description of the area.

Colonel Monro and General Howe are both buried in the narthex of St. Peter's Episcopal Church in Albany. Robert Rogers was not so lucky. His remains were disinterred after approximately 20 years and went to a charnel house, along with others to be rendered into soap or fertilizer.

Other members of the battle went on to become famous in their own right and the families live on today. Most notable is the current John Stark, who teaches school in Massachusetts, fighting for better education and writing a book about Benedict Arnold.

I had the good fortune to talk with a gentleman by the name of Ferguson, who works for the State of Illinois Department of Corrections. He is half Sioux and half Scot and clued me to the Indian thinking of that time. He pointed out that although some of the nations were warlike, most were not. They did not like to fight; but, if pushed to that point, they believed in hitting the enemy as hard and viciously as they could to bring a quick end to the conflict.

In the village of Fort Ticonderoga I met a couple, Joseph and Eleanor McBride, who provided me with yet another insight. Eleanor is of Native American and French ancestry. Her French forebears arrived in the area in 1755 and helped build Fort Ticonderoga. Some of their furniture is on display at the fort. While talking, I remarked that some 200-odd years ago, her family and mine were trying to kill each other for whatever the reason, yet we were talking and drinking coffee like old friends and neighbors. She laughed, agreed and pointed out that was 200 years ago. Now we are no longer French, Indian or British, we are Americans.

Maybe her answer was what the war was all about. An interesting point about the war was a song that is known to most American, Canadian and British children and is sung by each new generation. During the French and Indian War a young doctor by the name of Richard Shuckbury serving with General Abercrombie was amused by the carryings on of the young colonial recruits. He, as a result, wrote a tune which is known as "Yankee Doodle." As a friend of mine would say, "a piece of garbage can trivia," but interesting, nevertheless.

DRIVING TOUR: For anyone who is so inclined to want to visit "The Up-Down, Wet-Dry, Elongated Battleground," it is an easy one-day (or longer) excursion, depending on one's personal desires. Take Route 9 south from the village of Lake George (the location of Fort William Henry) past "Bloody Pond" and the site of the "Bloody Morning Scout" to Route 197. Turn left (east) on Route 197 leading to Fort Edward. You are basically using the old British Military Road. At Fort Edward turn right to head south at Route 22 and go about a quarter to a half mile and you will find the marker for old Fort Edward.

Returning to Route 22, you go north and come to Fort Anne. On the very north edge of town you will find a bank building constructed as a blockhouse. This is the reconstructed Fort Anne and it sits on the edge of Wood Creek. Whether the blockhouse is a correct reconstruction is something of a moot point as indications are that the original Fort Anne was a stockade.

From there, continue north on Route 22 through the village of Whitehall, birthplace of the U.S. Navy and onward across South Bay, up to the portage from Lake George to Lake Champlain, and you will come to the turnoff for Fort Ticonderoga, which is on a side road.

Returning once again to Route 22, turn right to go back to Route 9. Turn right at the intersection and go north on Route 9 to Route 17 which will lead to Crown Point. To return to Lake George reverse your route from Crown Point and head south on Route 9. From Ticonderoga to Lake George Route 9 follows the old Indian trail between the two points.

As I titled the chapter, this is a postscript. Thoughts that probably should have appeared in another chapter and some of the impressions, insights and trivia I have collected appear at this point. It rambles and why not? It is, after all, a postscript. I close with a question and an answer. You may and can draw your own conclusions.

Was the war worth it? Quite frankly, I cannot tell you even after 20 years' research. As always with history, fact and fiction blur at the edges. Research can sharpen up the edges to a point. Only those who lived in that time frame and suffered through the events can answer the question, but only from their narrow perspective of 3 or 4 feet; and they all are dead.

"Fort Ann Post," Glens Falls National Bank and Trust Company. The building is constructed to look like a blockhouse in commemoration of Fort Anne, known to the French as Fort de la Reine. Photograph courtesy of Bob Bearor.

Fort Ticonderoga. Upper and lower defense positions, entrance to parade ground and enlisted men's barracks.

Defensive inner wall at Fort Ticonderoga. Officers' quarters are at left. Enlisted men's barracks are to the right.

Drawbridge to demi-lune at Fort Ticonderoga. Walls provide a deadly trench for any attacker.

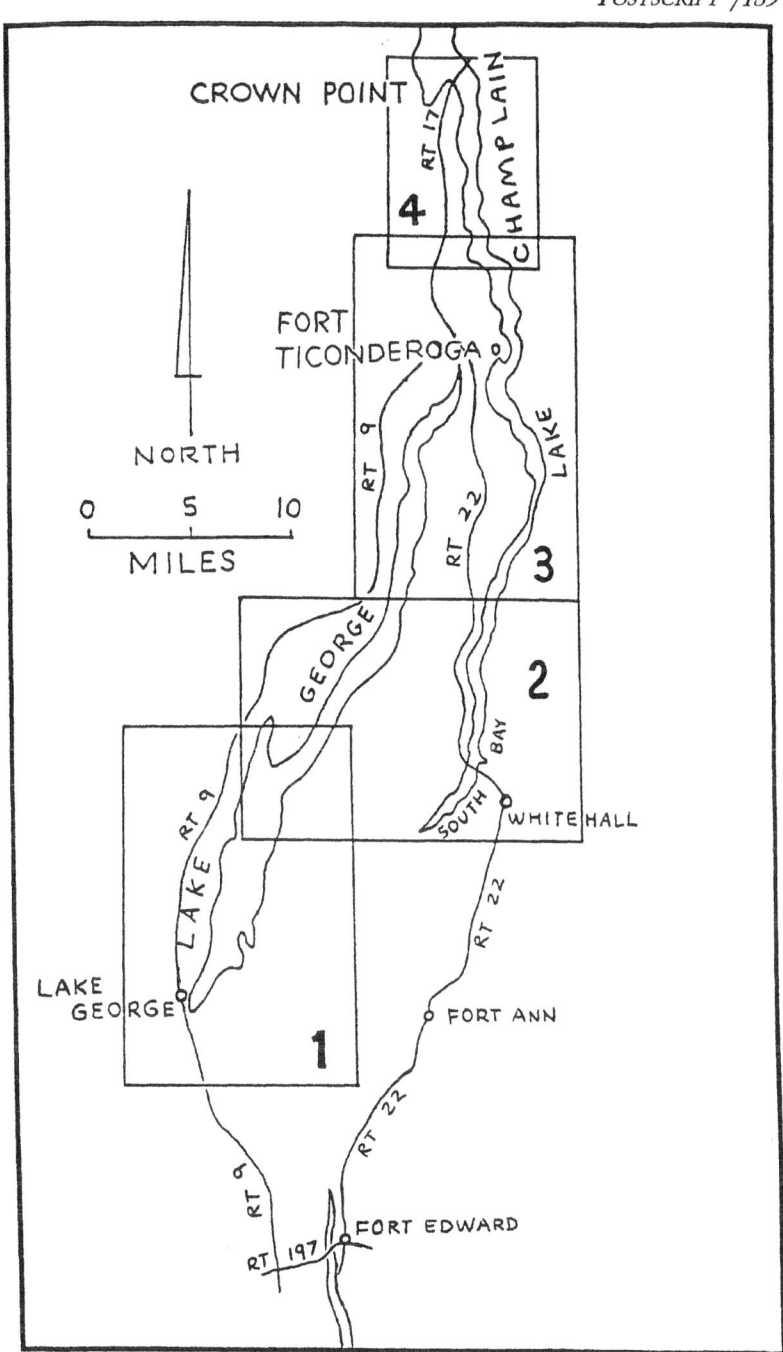

Key to Map figures for Driving Tour.

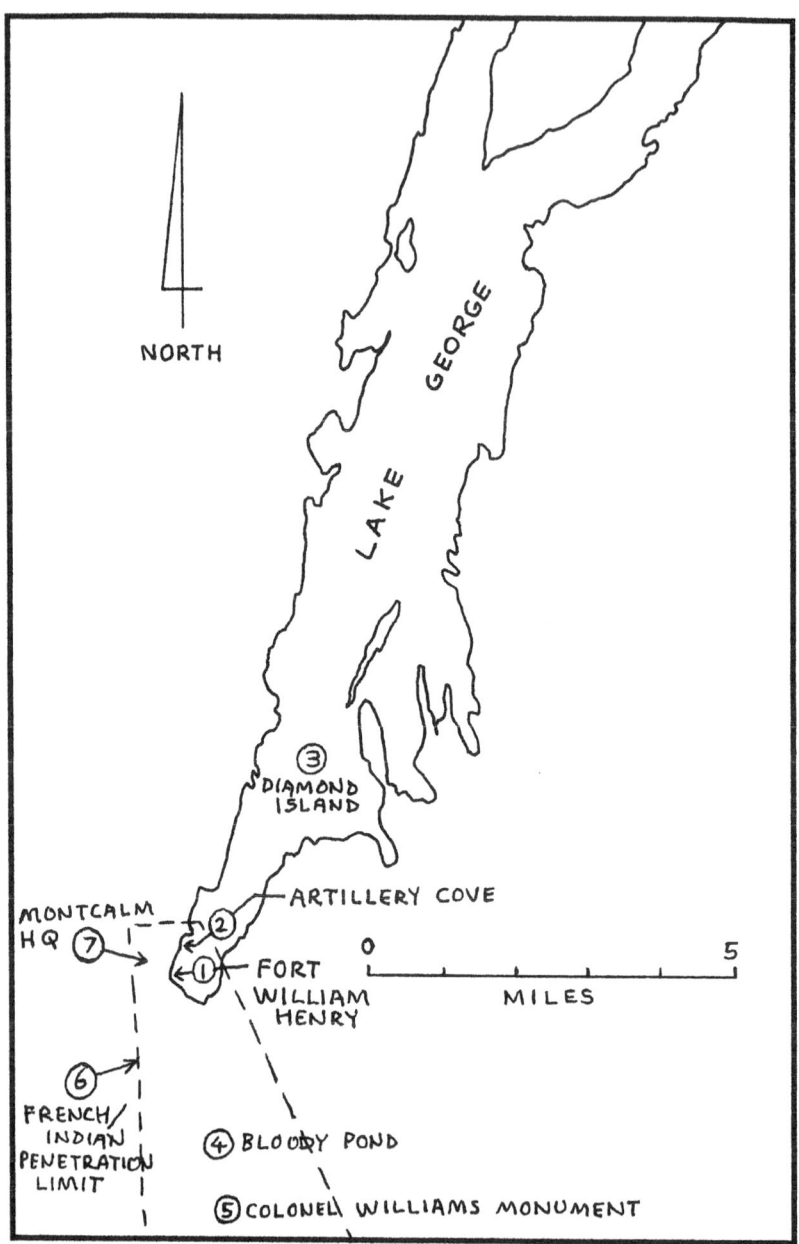

Map 1: Lake George at Fort William Henry. Note: Some sources locate Artillery Cove at Bolton, which is approximately 6.5 miles north of the fort. The time factor as established by Kilby's Journal would indicate the area indicated here.

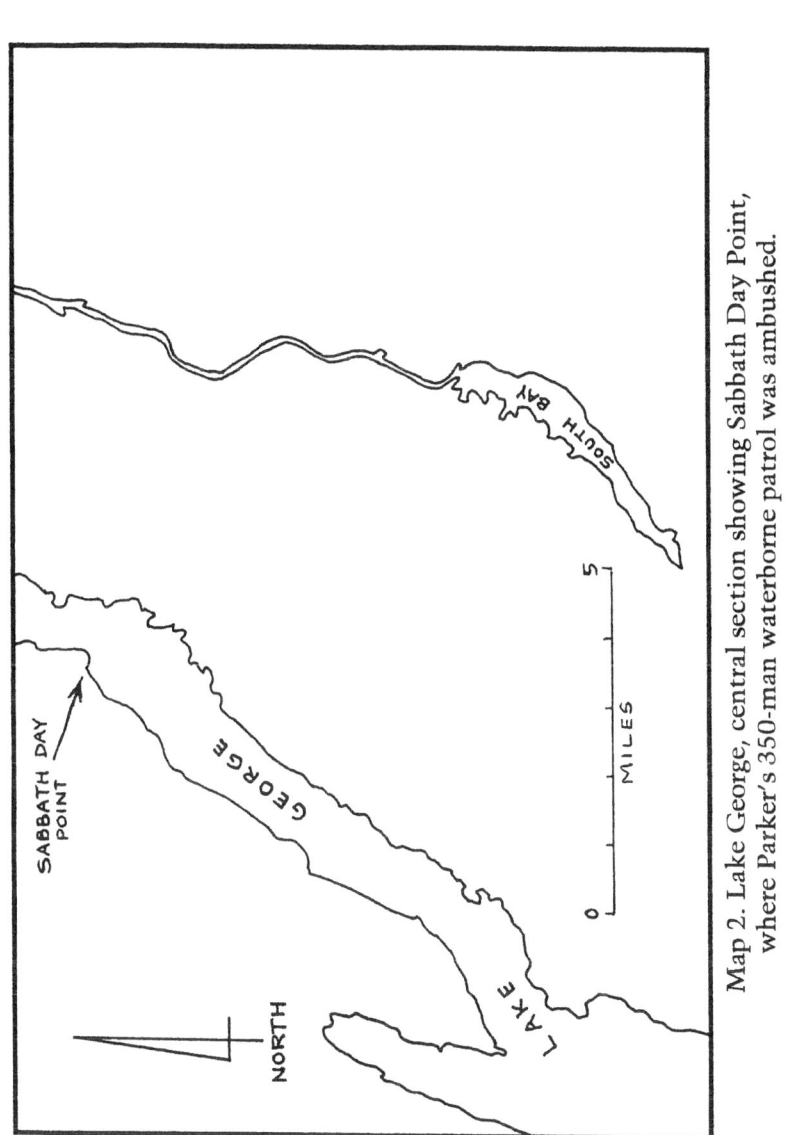

Map 2. Lake George, central section showing Sabbath Day Point, where Parker's 350-man waterborne patrol was ambushed.

142 / Relief Is Greatly Wanted

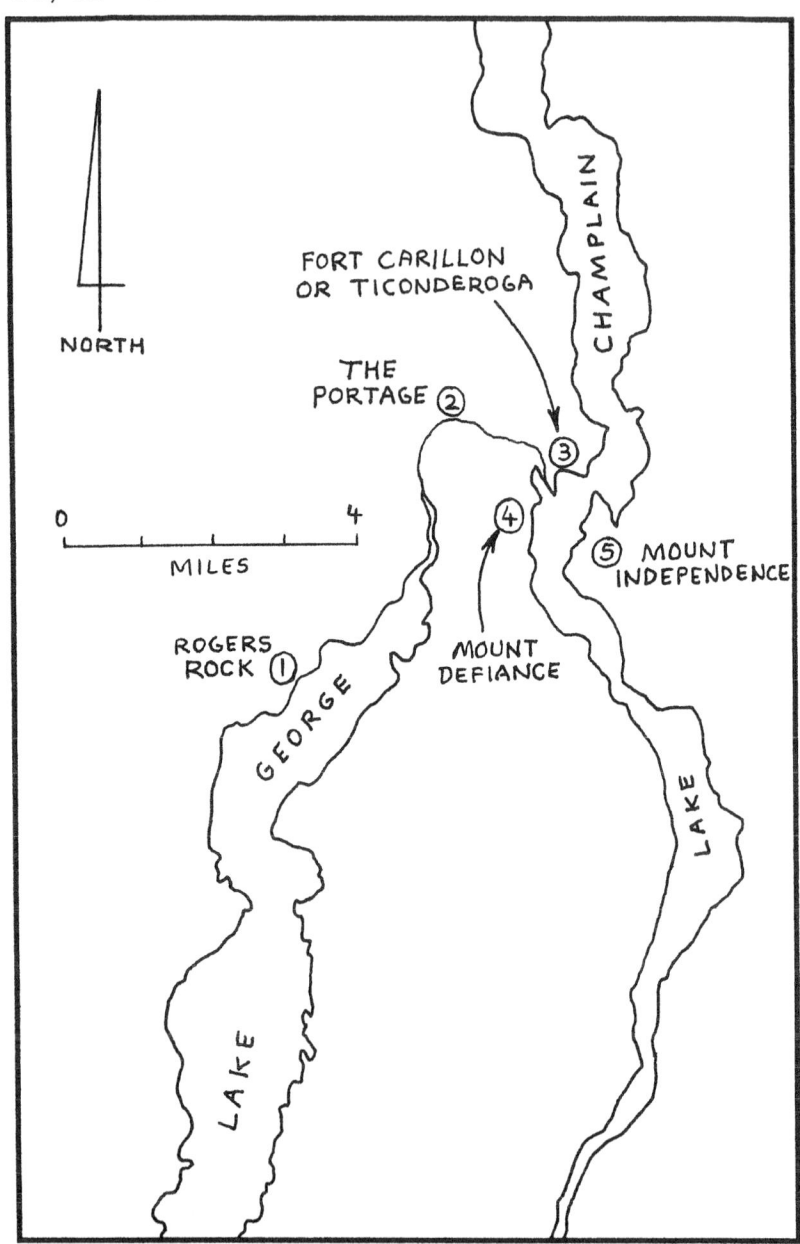

Map 3. Lake George at Ticonderoga. At the portage (2), several small streams were once channeled into one mill race to power the paper mills for the village of Ticonderoga. The actual portage is still there as it was constructed by nature. Mt. Defiance (4) and Mt. Independence (5) were used by the British forces to observe activities at Fort Ticonderoga.

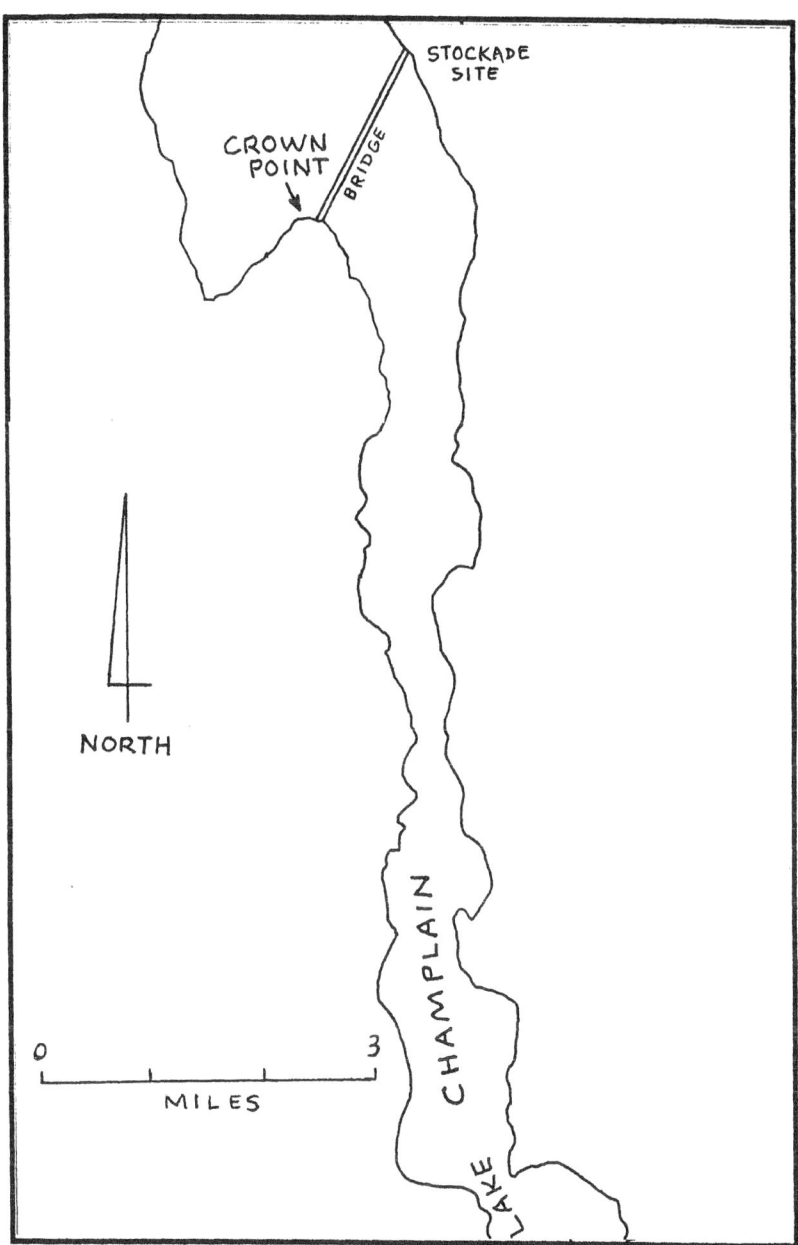

Map 4. Lake Champlain at Crown Point, or Fort St. Frederic (1). (2) Location of the original wooden stockade built by the French. Not one trace of it remains today.

Chapter Fifteen

EPILOGUE

For twelve years life in northern New York was quiet. It did not notice Pontiac's Rebellion other than sending a few militia volunteers. The rebellion was centered around Detroit, many miles to the west, and marked the year of 1763 as one of tremendous bloodshed and atrocity. Quite a few of the veterans of the French and Indian War, totally experienced in wilderness warfare, saw service at Detroit and the surrounding area. Rogers' Rangers took part in a great part of the fighting and sustained casualties that would devastate the families of northern New York due to death and injury. Although the French were no longer a threat, the Indians were still a problem, due to the loss of their land and the general indifference of the settlers.

Many of the British troops who were discharged in North America for economic reasons were presented land grants in the area of Fort Ticonderoga, along with colonists moving into more unsettled areas. Most of the land grants were on the east side of the lake from what is now Vermont into northern New York proper, slowly forming the villages and hamlets of Hubbardton, Whitehall, Fort Anne, and Fort Edward.

By 1775, Fort Ticonderoga was defended by little more than a "Corporal's Guard" and in a state of disrepair. Fort Anne had been reestablished as a fortified outpost and Fort George, at the site of former Fort William Henry, was little more than a rambling wreck.

Elsewhere, events were coming to a critical boiling point as "The Sons of Liberty" constantly harassed British officials and troops from Boston to New York. The Sons of Liberty were, as a group, composed of the very rich to the very poor, including some of the better known names in history.

The Australians have always been proud of their cultural history in that their ancestors were convicts, etc. North America was a penal colony, as well, with the population being composed of those who belonged to the "wrong" religion, debtors, those sent here to evade the wrath of outraged parents and spouses, and those in servitude due to court sentence and indenture. Many came from financially well-off families and were maintained by their families. This was the background of the Sons of Liberty. Their point of focus was that England was getting rich on the various taxes applied to goods furnished to the colonies and obtained from the colonies, and none of the money was being used for the good of the colonies. Somehow, the expense that England incurred to maintain the safety of the colonies did not occur to these individuals. As a result, unreasoned feelings boiled over into the revolution, which England did not want. New York again found itself living in fear of the silent arrow, war cry and scalping knife.

The war erupted at Fort Ticonderoga on 10 May 1775. Ethan Allen, Benedict Arnold and 83 members of the Vermont militia known as the "Green Mountain Boys," captured the fort. With the capture, they acquired 59 cannon, howitzers and mortars which were transported 200 miles through the wilderness by ox-drawn sleds to Cambridge, Massachusetts to be used against the British forces in Boston.

Leaving a detachment in Fort Ticonderoga, Allen proceeded south to Fort George, captured it and established a small garrison at the fort.

Ethan Allen was born in 1738 in, it is believed, Litchfield, Connecticut. He had a minimal education and was highly opinionated. He was extremely strong, had a taste for showy clothes and manners and a great volubility of speech. He fought in the French and Indian War and became involved in land speculation in 1770, fought in the expedition to Canada, was captured by the British in September 1775 and released in 1778. He was involved in politics for a while, retiring from same in 1784. He wrote "Narrative of Colonel Ethan Allen's Captivity" in 1779 and

"Reason the Only Oracle of Man" in 1784. He died in Burlington, Vermont, in 1789.

The colonists, or Americans as they were starting to call themselves, encouraged by their success at Fort Ticonderoga and Fort George, decided to attack Montreal and Quebec.

Brigadier General Richard Montgomery attacked Montreal. He succeeded in taking Montreal and then joined Benedict Arnold at Quebec where Montgomery was killed. Montgomery was born in 1738 in Swords County, Ireland. Educated at Trinity College, Dublin, he served in the British Army during the French and Indian War. He returned to England at the end of the war. He returned to North America in 1772 – settling near New York City. He married in 1773 and became a brigadier general in the Continental Army in 1775, dying at Quebec on 30 December 1775.

Benedict Arnold met with defeat at Quebec, retiring by boat down Lake Champlain, pursued by Sir Guy Carleton, governor general of Canada.

The pursuit would be a long, ongoing sea battle of epic stature on an inland lake most notably known for the "Battle of Valcour Island." Arnold would again know defeat, but save the majority of his command from capture by the British and their Indian allies. He beached his boats and burned them, escaping by fighting his way through Indian war parties across country to the safety of Crown Point.

During the same time frame Colonel "Mad" Anthony Wayne and his regiment of Pennsylvania militia were busy strengthening Fort Ticonderoga. Wayne was born in 1745 in Chester County, Pennsylvania. He organized and commanded a regiment in the Continental Army from Chester County. In 1776 he covered the retreat of Americans from Trois-Rivières after Arnold's failure at Quebec. During the winter of 1776-77 he commanded Fort Ticonderoga. He saw extended service during the Revolution and gained his most notoriety for his defeat of the Indians at the "Battle of Fallen Timbers" in Ohio Territory in August 1794. He died in 1796.

London, winter of 1776-77: King George, Lord Germain and General Burgoyne developed a three-part plan that would, hopefully, end the war in North America.

The plan was to send a large force up Lake Champlain to Fort Ticonderoga, from there to Albany where it would join with an army from New York City under the command of Lord Howe. Originally, Governor Carleton of Canada was to lead the army, but Burgoyne insisted he could do the job. Burgoyne had no experience in handling troops in the North American wilderness and did not know the country or the people.

The plan was set in motion from Canada. Burgoyne split his army, sending General Barry St. Leger up the St. Lawrence to the Oswego River and down that river through the Six Nations, gathering warriors from the Nations as he headed south toward the Mohawk Valley. Burgoyne headed down Lake Champlain. Lord Howe in New York City never got his orders to proceed up the Hudson to Albany and ended up engaged against General Washington at Brandywine.

At the time Burgoyne headed south Fort Ticonderoga was commanded by Major General Arthur St. Claire. He felt that the fort could be protected from a frontal assault. He was correct in this thinking as Montcalm had proved beyond all doubt that the fort could not be carried by frontal assault in 1759. Burgoyne did not try a frontal assault. He left the matter to his able artillery commander, Phillips, who put cannon on the heights of Mt. Defiance overlooking the fort. St. Claire evacuated the fort without firing a shot, using the eastern side of Lake Champlain with Burgoyne following closely.

St. Claire attempted to slow the British advance by destroying bridges and felling trees across the road. He lost skirmishes at Whitehall and Fort Anne. Burgoyne finally caught up with the Americans at Fort Edward where he defeated them and captured the fort. As Burgoyne enjoyed a certain amount of success in this phase of the attack, St. Leger was running into problems. He had proceeded to the headwaters of the Mohawk River and had begun a siege of Fort Stanwix – modern-day Rome, New York.

Arthur St. Claire was born in 1734 at Thurson, Caithness County, Scotland. He left the University of Edinburgh in 1757 to become an officer in the British army, served in the French and Indian War, resigned his commission in 1762 and settled in Pennsylvania. During the Revolution he served in the expedition to Canada as colonel of a regiment he raised in 1775. He was promoted to brigadier general and authorized to organize the New Jersey militia. As a major general he was given command of Fort Ticonderoga in 1777. He was court-martialed in 1778 for evacuating the fort and cleared of all charges. He served in the Continental Congress from 1785 to 1787. After leaving congress, he was appointed as the first governor of the Northwest Territory in 1787. In 1791 he became he commander-in-chief of the forces fighting the Indians. The Indians surprised and defeated him and he resigned his commission in 1792. A congressional investigation committee was appointed to examine his conduct against the Indians and found him blameless. President Thomas Jefferson removed him in 1802 as governor because of his arbitrary rule. He died impoverished in 1818.

As Fort Stanwix came under siege, word spread rapidly and locals under General Nicholas Herkimer quickly assembled to come to the aid of the fort. However, the hotheads would not listen to Herkimer's urge for caution and walked into an ambush known as the "Battle of Oriskany." Among Herkimer's forces were Oneida, Tuscaroras and 13 Mohawks from Canada. The British ambush force was composed of Loyalists, Senecas, and Mohawks. The battle was one of the fiercest and bloodiest battles of the Revolution. It created an irreparable split within the Six Nations. The split had been foretold by the Iroquois prophet, Deganawidah when the Six Nations of Iroquois Confederacy was founded. He told the Confederacy that it would last until the ashes of the council fire blew into their eyes and the Confederacy would cease to exist.

Nicholas Herkimer was born in 1728 near present day Herkimer, New York, probably in the village of German Flats. He served in the French and Indian War and was appointed a brigadier general, New York militia in 1776. He died as a result of a wound he received at Oriskany Creek in 1777 while defeating the enemy force.

German Flats is of some interest to the author as his maternal grandmother was born a Bartz and her mother a Dietz. Both families lived in German Flats when it was raided by the French and Indians on Sunday, 13 November 1757, by a French and Indian force estimated at 800. Although exact casualty figures are unknown, there were three survivors in the Dietz family. This author came very close to never existing.

Although under siege, Fort Stanwix had its share of excellent soldiers. A sortie from the fort created panic and confusion among the Indians and loyalists or Tories in St. Leger's force. The sortie captured the majority of the Indian supplies, which would cost the Indians dearly in the forthcoming winter. St. Leger, through personality, was able to salvage enough of his force to tighten his siege of Fort Stanwix. He felt so sure, or perhaps unsure, of his position that he demanded surrender of the fort.

Two volunteers, one of whom was Benedict Arnold, slipped out of Fort Stanwix and headed to Albany to request reinforcements. Arnold was put in charge of the relief column. On his return trip, he stopped at German Flats and learned there were some British prisoners, one was a Yost Schuyler, a mentally handicapped young man who was forever loyal to his king. His mother asked Arnold to save his life as he was sentenced to be hanged as a traitor. Arnold agreed to spare the boy and his brother, if he would go to St. Leger and tell him that a great army was on the way from Albany to relieve Fort Stanwix.

Schuyler agreed to the terms. His coat was hung on a bush and several bullets fired through it. He then ran toward the British lines with the Americans chasing him and firing at him, although not close enough to hurt him.

Schuyler ran into one of the Iroquois camps and told the Indians that an army fully as many as the leaves in the forest was on the way from Albany. The Indians were already demoralized due to Oriskany and its associated prophecy. Schuyler's story put them into a panic and they fled, helping themselves to British supplies. St. Leger realized he was in an untenable position and left behind the Indians, leaving tents, artillery and stores.

Burgoyne was at Schuylerville. He found he was short of dragoon mounts for his German dragoons and having intelligence that there were mounts and stores available at Bennington, Vermont, as well as people loyal to the crown in that area, he dispatched a small force of German troops, Indians and loyalists to obtain the horses and supplies.

John Stark, former Ranger captain and one of the defenders of Bunker Hill in Boston, now a general, engaged the British force and defeated it. Burgoyne, now knowing that neither St. Leger nor Lord Howe were to be of help, was very much on his own. He was surrounded on all sides by the Americans, cut off from Canada, and his Indian allies deserted him because of his indifferent attitude toward their dead and wounded. His Canadian militia were deserting as well. His only apparent reaction was "Britons never recede."

One of the worst aspects of Burgoyne's advance was that his Indian allies, known as "Burgoyne's Hyenas" were killing innocent people, mostly women and children, and taking scalps. The one incident that set the Americans on edge was the massacre of Jane McCrea. She was visiting friends in Fort Edward, hoping to see the young man with whom she was in love. He was an officer in the British army. As Burgoyne got close to Fort Edward, she decided to follow her brother's advice and go to Albany. As she was preparing to leave, Burgoyne's Indians descended on the house where she was staying and captured her. As she was being led away, she was killed; one story claims she was accidentally shot by an American patrol trying to rescue her. The other story states she was killed out-of-hand by the Indians. Her scalp was taken, although it was recovered later by her British officer. He left the army and returned to Canada. Their two graves are inside a fenced plot in a cemetery on the south side of Fort Edward.

Burgoyne had moved south from Fort Edward, advancing on Albany. He held up at present-day Schuylerville, old Saratoga. The Americans were at Bemis Heights, a short distance away. The American commander was General Horatio Gates. Burgoyne had in his command two excellent leaders, General Hugh Fraser and Baron Reidesel, commander of the German troops. He also had allowed his officers to bring their wives and children with them. For all appearances, it was a large picnic gathering. Finally, Burgoyne's troops started moving and were spotted by General Benedict Arnold. He sent a request to Gates for support and attempted to turn the British right, while at the same time the British, under General Fraser, attempted to turn the American left. Arnold almost accomplished what he set out to do. He would have carried the day and the battle if Gates had sent the requested reinforcements. The British did send reinforcements and they carried the day, which has now, in hindsight become listed as a draw.

Gates was extremely jealous of Arnold and even went so far as to relieve him of his command. The reason for the jealousy is not really known, but it was the first step toward Arnold eventually deserting to the British.

For the next two weeks the two armies reinforced their positions and sniped at each other. Baron Reidesel had a house built for his wife and daughters as the weather was getting colder. On 7 October 1777, the Baroness planned to give a dinner for Burgoyne and his officers. Troops in small parties were sent out to forage for food and found a field of oats which they started to gather for the army's horses. The Americans opened fire on the foraging parties, which rapidly turned into a full-blown battle, with hand-to-hand fights taking place along the line. Arnold was in the thick of it, fighting as a private solder. His presence stirred the Americans, as did that of General Daniel Morgan.

Major-General John Burgoyne. Published by kind permission of the Council of The Army Historical Research Society and the National Army Museum.

General Fraser was in the front lines encouraging his troops with great success. Arnold and Morgan, although both knowing and respecting him, felt he had to be removed. Morgan ordered one of his sharpshooters to shoot Fraser. The intent from what hindsight can determine was to wound him and remove him from the line. Unfortunately, it proved to be a death-dealing wound. At his funeral the next day the Americans mistook the procession for an attack party and fired on it. Finally, realizing their error, they stopped shooting at the processions. After that they fired minute guns in honor of this fine soldier.

The British army lost heart. As the British started pulling back, Arnold was wounded in the leg. As Burgoyne started back to Fort Edward, the weather turned bad and the road became a river of mud. Finally, on 17 October 1777, Burgoyne surrendered to the Americans. With the surrender, the British lost just under 6,000 troops, 42 cannon, and a multitude of arms and ammunition.

General John Burgoyne was born in 1722, served in the Seven Years' War and was elected to Parliament in 1768. He helped reform the East India Company's rule of India. On his first trip to the colonies he arrived in Boston in 1775 with reinforcements for General Gage, and witnessed the Battle of Bunker Hill before joining Sir Guy Carleton in Canada in 1776. He returned to England in that same year and came back to Canada in 1777. He was defeated at Saratoga on 17 October 1777. He returned to England again in 1782 and was appointed commander-in-chief of Ireland. He gained notoriety as a playwright. He was the soldier's friend and referred to the Americans as "rabble in arms." He died in 1792.

Horatio Gates was born in Malden, Essex, England in 1727. He fought in the French and Indian War and saw service in Martinique, resigned from the British army in 1772 and settled in West Virginia. During the Revolution, he joined the Continental Army as a general, saw service in Boston and was commander of troops during the Battle of Saratoga in 1777.

At one time he was considered a serious rival of Washington as commander-in-chief. In June 1780 he was appointed commander in the Carolinas. He was defeated at Camden in 1780 and left in disgrace. He moved to New York in 1790 and died in 1806.

Daniel Morgan was born in New Jersey in 1736, saw service in the French and Indian War, and assumed command in Quebec after Arnold was wounded. Morgan was captured and exchanged in 1776, and saw service in Saratoga. After the war he served as U. S. Congressman.

Shortly after Burgoyne's surrender, General James Clinton led a force from New York as far as Ticonderoga in pursuit of Sir John Johnson, son of Sir William Johnson, who had been raiding down the Mohawk Valley. Johnson escaped to Canada. Johnson, with a force of 500 Tories and Indians, had attacked and destroyed the villages of Johnstown, Canajoharie and Middleburg.

A British force from Canada attacked Fort George with the fight taking place very near the "Bloody Pond" from French and Indian War fame. The Americans lost and Fort George fell to the British.

James Clinton was born in Orange County, New York in 1773. He was the brother of George Clinton, American statesman and father of DeWitt Clinton, who would become governor of New York. He served in the French and Indian War in the Quebec Campaign and was involved in the futile defense of Fort Clinton in the Hudson Valley. He also served with General John Sullivan in his expedition against the Indians and served at Yorktown. He died in 1812.

Sir John Johnson was born in the Mohawk Valley, New York in 1742. His father was Sir William Johnson. He fought in Pontiac's Rebellion and for his services was knighted in 1765. Like his brother-in-law, Guy Johnson, he attempted to organize the settlers and Indians of the Mohawk region against the patriots. The plan failed and he fled to Montreal. He served with St. Leger and fought at Oriskany in 1777. He led several raids in the Mohawk and Schoharie Valleys. After the war he moved to Canada and in

1782 succeeded Guy Johnson as Superintendent of Indian Affairs.

By early 1778 most of New York was free of major battles involving uniformed armies. They were not free of raids and massacres by Tories and Indians under the direction of Guy Johnson, Sir John Johnson, Colonel John Butler, his son Walter; or by the Seneca war chief Cornplanter and the Mohawk war chief Joseph Brant.

John Butler was born in New London, Connecticut in 1728. He served in the French and Indian War and distinguished himself at the battle for Fort Niagara in 1759. He joined the British during the Revolution and became deputy to Guy Johnson at Fort Niagara, fought with St. Leger in his move down the Mohawk Valley and organized Butler's Rangers who, with his son Walter, he led in raid upon outlying settlements. He raided Wyoming Valley in 1778 and was unable to control his Indian allies from the ensuing massacre. He later acknowledged taking 227 scalps and burning over 1,000 homes.

Guy Johnson was born in Ireland in 1740. He came to North America as a boy. He served in the French and Indian War. Guy married a daughter of Sir William Johnson in 1763. He served as deputy to Sir William from 1762 until succeeding him as Superintendent of Indian Affairs in 1764. He joined he British in the Revolution, helping to keep most of the Iroquois loyal to the British. His headquarters was at Fort Niagara from 1779 to 1791. With his deputy, John Butler, he directed raids against frontier settlements. He died in 1788.

Joseph Brant was born Thayendanega in 1742. His sister Molly would marry Sir William Johnson. Brant saw service in the French and Indian War under Sir William. In 1761 he was sent to Eleazar Wheelock's Indian School in Lebanon, Connecticut. This school would later become Dartmouth College. Brant also received further education in England. He saw service under Sir William during Pontiac's Rebellion in 1763. He stayed loyal to the British in the Revolution and fought at Oriskany in 1777. He was one of the leaders during the Cherry Valley Raid and possibly involved in the Wyoming Valley Raid. (Although the facts would support that, time and distance would say no.) After the Cherry Valley Raid, a kidnapped baby was returned to its mother by Brant, along with a note stating that he did not make war on women and children. In another instance, he entered a cabin in Cherry Valley and put his mark on the forehead of the woman and her children, saving them and their home. They were in fact Tories, but that would not have saved them without Brant's help.

After the Revolution, as he could get no settlement to the Indian land in question, he moved his people to Canada where he received land and subsidies for them. He was a strong Christian, a missionary and translated the Book of Common Prayer and the Gospel of Mark into Mohawk.

He would, with his Mohawks, attack the Oneidas and come close to wiping out the tribe for their staying with the Americans and for the losses they inflicted on the other tribes at Oriskany. He died in 1807.

Cornplanter was born in 1740, the half-breed son of an Albany trader. He acquired great influence among the Senecas. During the Revolution he led multiple raids against the Americans. Later he favored friendship with the Americans and signed the Treaty of Fort Stanwix in 1784. He died in 1836.

The raids on Cherry Valley and Wyoming Valley caused George Washington to order a punitive expedition against the Iroquois.

The expedition was commanded by General John Sullivan. The actual date of the expedition was during the summer of 1779. Sullivan with able assistance from General Clinton, destroyed the Iroquois lands as far west as the Genesee Valley. It has been estimated that some 43 Indian villages were burned and some 160,000 bushels of corn destroyed by fire or were being cut down. Immense orchards of apple, peach and pear trees were cut down and burned. Because of this expedition, Washington would be known to the Iroquois as "The Town Destroyer."

John Sullivan was born in Somersworth, New Hampshire in 1740. He was educated as a lawyer and served on the

Continental Congress from 1774 to 1775 and again from 1780 to 1781. He fought in the Revolution, serving at Boston and later during the Battle of Long Island. He was captured by the British. He was exchanged and fought at Trenton, Princeton, Brandywine and Germantown. In 1778, he fought with the French Fleet at Newport, Rhode Island, in a joint land/sea operation. His land operation was successful, but the naval attack failed. In 1779 with General Clinton he undertook a punitive expedition against the Iroquois and the "Butlers." Butler was defeated and the Iroquois lands were laid to waste. He was elected Chief Executive of New Hampshire in 1786, 1787 and 1789. He was influential in getting the Constitution ratified.

The Revolutionary War finally ended in 1783. From 1778 to 1783 Tory and Indian raids became extremely rare and finally stopped altogether. New York, after 174 years of unbelievable agony, knew peace. That peace was ratified between the Iroquois and whites with the signing of the Treaty of Fort Stanwix in 1784.

Relief was finally granted.

Major Robert Rogers. *Fort Ticonderoga Museum.*

Chapter Sixteen

HIS MAJESTY'S INDEPENDENT COMPANY OF RANGERS

Probably no single military organization has received more attention than His Majesty's Independent Company of Rangers, better known as Rogers' Rangers. This group of men has, over the years, inspired books, short stories, a television series, movies, plays, reenactment groups and during World War II the resurrection of the unit under the name "Darby's Rangers" and later the Rangers of the U. S. Army. Their exploits are known throughout the modern world. Indeed it would be safe to say that every elite fighting force in the modern world can point to Rogers' Rangers as their ancestor unit.

The Rangers were the basis of the "Explorer" program of the Boy Scouts of America and Robert Rogers' exploits formed the basis for James Fenimore Cooper's *Leatherstocking Tales*. John R. Cuneo in his book, *Robert Rogers of the Rangers* did an outstanding job of detailing Rogers' life. Kenneth Roberts in his book, *Northwest Passage*, provided us with a semi-fictional account of Rogers' raid on the Abenaki Village of St. Francis, Canada. For those of us who have seen the movie, Spencer Tracy will forever by Robert Rogers. In truth, what few paintings are available of Rogers, show a marked resemblance between the two men.

The Rangers evolved from what were called scouting companies. The companies varied in size, but usually never exceeded 50 members serving under a designated captain. Their function was what the name implied. Eventually, they would become known as Ranging companies and from that simply Rangers. They had no designated uniform and usually wore homespun or deerskin clothing or a combination thereof. They carried a firelock, hatchet, knife and the officers a compass. Their pack was a rolled blanket and sometimes a bearskin. They were all volunteers and were, with rare exception, expert shots and could live off the land, read trail signs like others read a book, were extremely knowledgeable in the art of cover and concealment and had no qualms about fighting the Indian on his own terms.

They knew their chances and knew if captured faced the most horrible type of death the Indian could devise. Robert Rogers would see the Rangers brought to the peak of perfection. He selected his initial company commanders from men that he personally knew from a lifetime on the frontier fighting Hurons and, in particular, the Abenaki. These men, in turn, selected the men for their companies from the men they knew and trusted. The junior officers and NCO's were elected by the men in the companies and the result was one of the most well-disciplined and highly-motivated units in His Majesty's forces.

Ranger tactics have always been very simple and direct. To put them in the simplest form possible; get in quietly without being discovered, do the job, get out fast and, if engaged by the enemy, use a predetermined cutout and meeting place.

The Rangers had an all-Indian detachment of Stockbridge Mohigans. Rogers trusted them implicitly as they had taught him the skills that made him so successful. The leaders were Checkaunkum and his son Naunauptaunk, better known as Captain Jacobs The Elder and Captain Jacobs. Cooper would change their names to Chingachgook and Uncas. There was, in reality, an Uncas, but he was a Pequot born in 1588. The real Uncas was trouble for both Indian and English alike. He was brother-in-law to Sassacus, the great Sachem of the Pequot. He sold out the Pequot and lived out his life with the Mohawks, dying in 1683. In real life Captain Jacobs The Elder lived to a fairly advanced age and Naunauptaunk was captured by the Huron and killed.

The Rangers were highly regarded by the regular army and militia, but from something of a stand-off distance. At Fort Edward, their quarters were on an island on the Hudson, which is now known as Ranger or Rogers Island. At Fort William Henry, they had their own picquetted camp to the west of the fort proper. They would, as history has shown, have to fight two withdrawal actions from that camp and by the time the second was over, they were less than happy campers.

Lieutenant Colonel Gage of the 80th Light Infantry would have his unit trained in Ranger tactics, but never gaining the assignments or recognition that the Rangers did, he would become Rogers' nemesis for the rest of Rogers' life, trying both successfully and unsuccessfully to besmirch Rogers in any form he could.

A great many regular army types would volunteer for the Rangers, giving up the red uniform for deerskin or homespun and later the forest green uniform of the Rangers.

There were changes in personnel due to death and wounds, and end of enlistment. Many names do not show on the various rosters I have seen. Three names that did not appear as enlisted were Sergeant Caleb Dodge, and Privates Josiah and Jonathan Dodge. Three officers show up only in after-action reports or dispatches. One of them, Captain McGinnis; is truly a mystery as it is not known if he was a captain from the Hampshire militia or, as alleged by Kenneth Roberts, an officer from the regular army. Captain Jacob Abbott was militia and Captain William Symer was probably militia.

The Rangers saw action where they were needed. Their primary locale was around Lakes George and Champlain during the life of Fort William Henry. Later it would change to Lake Champlain and the St. Lawrence River watershed as far east as Louisbourg. From 1756 to 1758/59 they were based at Fort Edward and after 1759 they were based out of Crown Point or what had been the French fort – St. Frederic.

During the month of January 1758 the Rangers were issued a dark green uniform. The uniform consisted of a short sleeveless jacket with wings such as worn by drummers, waistcoat with sleeves, drawers, gaiters, tricorn hat for parade and a tam for field work. Jacket and waistcoat were lined with green serge, collars and cuffs contrasting to the coarse woolen frieze of the jacket and waistcoat. A shirt was worn under the waistcoat. Buttons were white metal. Officers had silver lace on button holes and edges. Drawers were linen or canvas. Gaiters brown like those worn by the regular units – buttoning from mid thigh to ankle. Footwear was either army issue boots or moccasins.

Officers' tricorns were trimmed with silver lace. In the field officers wore a tricorn cropped to leave only a skull covering with a turned-up flap in front – a variant of the dragoon helmet – with silver lace, crown and script on the front flap and a soft black horsehair plume centered on the top of the hat. Other ranks and NCO's wore a dark green tam with an evergreen twig or feather stuck on the side or back.

Weapons were standard army issue as were haversacks and canteens. Belts and shot pouches were brown leather. Blankets were carried in horseshoe rolls unless worn for warmth.

As well as having the most unique uniform in the army, the Rangers had their own unique trademark. The army used a standard single round load, on occasion a double load. The Rangers used a load of one standard ball and six to eight rounds of pea shot. Under a hundred yards this defoliated the area and was deadly.

Robert Rogers is still a man of mystery. Much is known about him, yet to this day his reputation suffers greatly from comments and deliberate efforts to destroy the man and his character.

He was raised on the frontier under the most trying of circumstances, yet his writings reflect an agile, brilliant mind which could grasp the situation at hand quickly and find the most logical solution. His handwriting is neat, crisp, quite well-punctuated, and his spelling is that of an educated man.

It has been said that as an ordinary man well met, you would probably feel sorry for him; but, as a soldier and leader of men, few were his equal. His Rangers believed in him and would follow him anywhere, no matter the odds. In fact they followed his leadership, direct and indirect, through some 27 battles and 44 recorded scouts during the period 1755 to 1761, no mean feat in any age.

Robert Rogers was born 18 November 1731 in Methuen, Massachusetts the fourth son of James Rogers, Sr. and Mary McFatridge. When he was nine years of age, the family moved to a farm about 16 miles from present-day Concord, New Hampshire. He was Ulster Scot by parentage and through everyday life on the frontier and a close friendship with the Stockbridge Mohigans who lived in the area, a very excellent scout and Indian fighter by the age of thirteen.

He saw service during King George's War as a scout with the scouting company of Captain Daniel Ladd and later with the scout company of Ebenezer Eastman. His dislike of the Abenaki was greatly enhanced when they destroyed the family farm with the exception of one apple tree in 1748.

He saw service with both the Massachusetts and New Hampshire regiments and during the same period was arrested on suspicion of counterfeiting printed tender. He was eventually determined to be more the victim than wrongdoer and proceeded on with his life as did a childhood friend by the name of Carver. Carver would live through the siege of Fort William Henry, leave a short narrative of same and eventually assist in the mapping of what is now Minnesota and Wisconsin.

In April 1755, he was commissioned captain of the Ranger Company of Blanchard's New Hampshire regiment.

In August 1755, he and his company were detached to serve under Sir William Johnson at Fort Edward and the Rangers became a fact of history.

Rogers lived by the code of the era, an eye for an eye. Once he killed an Indian baby by bashing its head against a tree. He had seen the Indians do it often enough, or the results thereof. When called on it, he replied, "It was a nit and if I allowed it to live, it would become a louse."

From the year 1761, Rogers' life became what can only be termed confusing. He became a close friend of Sir William Johnson, would fight with Governor Shirley of Massachusetts about monies due for maintenance of the Rangers and run the same course with New Hampshire. He had already earned the dislike of Lieutenant Colonel (later General) Gage and, as previously indicated this dislike would pursue him for the balance of his days.

Apparently, after the French and Indian War, Rogers retired at half pay in New Hampshire. Conversely, we know that he made an expedition to Detroit and ably assisted in the defense of Detroit during Pontiac's War. In 1761 he married Elizabeth Brown and saw duty in South Carolina where he was again plagued by financial problems. In 1765 he was in London and is alleged to have captured a highwayman who attempted to rob a coach he was riding in. He is known to have presented a memorial to the King's Council urging a search for the Northwest Passage.

He wrote and had published in some three months his "Journals and Concise Account of North America." Shortly thereafter he was appointed governor of Michillimackinac. In December 1765 he completed his play, "Ponteach," and sailed for America.

Arriving in New York in January 1766, he received his commission and instructions for Michillimackinac from his old nemesis, General Gage. On his way to Michillimackinac he took part in Sir William Johnson's Indian conference at Oswego.

Rogers' Rangers Muster Roll for 23 July 1756 to 27 September 1756. This item is reproduced by permission of *The Huntington Library, San Marino, California.* Loudon Collection, LO2747.

—	Robert Rogers		William Stark
	Increase Moor		Nathaniel Martin
1st	Edward Crofton	7th	Joshua Martin
	William Morris		Hugh Sterling
	Noah Wright		
			Jonathan Brewer
	John Stark		Samuel Shepherd
2d	Robert Fletcher	8th	Joseph Waite
	Simon Stephens		Samuel Hamelton
	Eliab Brewer		
			Jonathan Burbank
	John Shepherd		Stephen Hoyt
3d	James Veil	9th	Partridge Hamelton
	Samuel Gilman		Andrew Ross
	Moses Kelsy		John McDuffy
		10th	Charles Rogers
	Charles Bulkley		Perry
4th	Henry Phillips		Archibald Stark
	Peter Bulkley		Thomas Lawrance
	John Dinsmoor	11th	William Holdan
			Andrew Willson
	John McCurdy		Engelbertus Horst
	Moses Hezon		Moses Brewer
5th	William Moor	12th	Porter
	Joseph Bolton		Joseph Johnston, Indian Warrior
			Joseph Duquipe
	James Rogers		
	Joseph Senter		
6th	Benjamin Fossit		
	Gregory McDonnell		

Muster Roll of Rogers' Rangers Officers of the 12 Ranger Companies. This item is reproduced by permission of *The Huntington Library, San Marino, California.* Loudon Collection, LO5379.

Muster Roll of Rogers' Rangers Officers of the 12 Ranger Companies - Corrections. This item is reproduced by permission of *The Huntington Library, San Marino, California.* Loudon Collection, LO5389A.

He finally arrived at Michillimackinac with his wife Elizabeth and his secretary Nathaniel Potter in August 1766. That same month he sent an expedition into the Mississippi watershed under a J. Tute, which included his old civilian and Ranger friend Carver.

The expedition was to map the area in the expectation that Rogers would be given orders to search for the Northwest Passage. This was an undying passion of Rogers', that a Northwest Passage did exist.

All was quiet until June 1767 when Benjamin Roberts arrived as Superintendent of Indian Trade. He and Rogers immediately clashed over the alleged overruns on withdrawal of funds. Rogers sent Roberts back to Gage on an insubordination charge. By December 1767, Gage ordered Rogers confined in irons until he could be sent to Montreal to face what turned out to be trumped up charges of treason. Rogers was supposed to have been dealing with either the French or Spanish for them to take over Michillimackinac. He was found not guilty of charges in October 1768.

In 1769 he sailed to England, received an audience with George III and received 3000 pounds sterling. He also took the time to bring suit against Gage for assault and imprisonment. By June 1770 his creditors had him thrown into Fleet Prison for not paying his debts. He petitioned the king twice from prison, once to obtain a commission in the East India Company which was rejected out of hand, and once to discover the Northwest Passage.

Finally, in June 1773 his brother James gave bond for his debts and he was released from prison. From July 1773 until March 1775 he is alleged to have served the Dey of Algiers. In April 1775 he was again in London petitioning for an appointment in India. Again, with no success. He then took the first ship bound for North America and landed in Maryland.

From this point until his death, his life has been related by various sources with so many unanswered questions that it is not absolutely certain what his thinking was. That he was badly hurt in the emotional sense and his character so besmirched he quite literally may have sustained an emotional, if not nervous, breakdown as well.

The most accurate information comes from a historical essay by Lorenzo Sabine in Volume II of *Biographical Sketches of Loyalists of the American Revolution*, published by Little, Brown and Company in Boston in 1864. It must be taken with a grain of salt as there is at least circumstantial evidence to counter some of Sabine's statements. It must be kept in mind that The Sons of Liberty were the foundation of the American Revolution. They were a cross cut of the lower, middle and upper classes. The upper class were some of the most well-known names in American history, including George Washington. The basis for the Sons of Liberty was simply that as a group they wanted their share of the taxes, tariffs and revenues levied by Lord North.

Not a few of the Sons of Liberty were Masons and had unbroken lines of communication throughout British-controlled North America. A good many of these individuals had no liking for Rogers as he was outspoken. To add to that, they had willingly left him in debt for monies owed for the maintenance of the Rangers. Others did not like him as he was not gentry born, yet had risen at various times to social position and contacts they never had or would ever have.

Circumstantial evidence tends to indicate that because of either personal or implanted suspicion, Washington was willing to make him a scapegoat to protect a spy that Washington had inside the Loyalist organization. This individual was a shoemaker by trade and was born Enoch Crosby. He was also known as Levi Foster, John Smith and John and Jacob Brown. He would eventually end up serving under the Marquis de Lafayette as a sergeant. It is a disputed issued whether he was the model for James Fenimore Cooper's hero in *The Spy*.

There is no question but what he and Rogers were in the same general vicinity at the same time and the "Committee for Detecting and Defeating Conspiracies" was going to protect their agent at all costs.

Washington also had a very active spy network in New York being operated by Abraham Woodhull, Benjamin Tallmadge, Robert Townsend and James Rivington. As the network operated within one of the biggest British posts, it was imperative that their identity be kept secret. Rogers would spend a great deal of time in New York attempting to tie down some land grants.

Enoch Crosby spent most of his time in Kingsbridge, White Plains, Fishkill, Marlboro and Pauling, New York, which are located between New York City and Albany and through which Rogers would have traveled.

When Rogers arrived in Maryland, he was basically a forgotten man as he had been out of the country for quite some time and the French and Indian War was old history. He also was out of touch with the political scene and, like most soldiers, really did not care about politics. Further, he was as ever his own man and did not like being pushed by anything or anyone. His primary concern was his financial problems and getting home to New Hampshire to see his family and friends.

His arrival was noted, but he was basically a retired British major on half pay and an old man. He proceeded to New Hampshire and while there called on Eleazer Wheelock, founder of Dartmouth College, to talk to him about some land grants for the college.

Prior to ever getting to New Hampshire, Rogers had been arrested in Philadelphia because of his retired status and released as the Continental Congress felt his only crime was being a retired officer. Arriving in New York and getting ready to leave for Albany he had a recurrence of his malaria (from his days in the Carolinas).

Dr. Wheelock apparently was aware of this and, in fact, Rogers made no secret of it. However, Wheelock misread Rogers' intent and wrote General Washington on 13 November 1775 that Rogers had visited him and in discussion had related that he had been offered a commission in the Continental Army, but because of his retired status had turned it down. Wheelock also advised that he had been informed by two soldiers that Rogers was second-in-command under British General Carleton in Canada.

Leaving Wheelock, Rogers visited his wife Elizabeth and his son Arthur and proceeded to Medford near Boston and requested leave to pass through the lines without hindrance as, "I have leave to retire on my half pay, and never expect to be called into the service again. I love North America, and I intend to spend the evening of my days in it."

Because of the suspicions that Wheelock had stirred up, Rogers was questioned quite closely by General John Sullivan at Washington's direction. The result was that nothing could be found wrong and Wheelock's letter could not be substantiated.

Rogers arrived in New York, but was ordered out of New York by William Alexander, Lord Sterling, who was an American general. Rogers headed to Philadelphia to seek a commission in the Continental Army, but was turned down because of his half pay status.

Rogers, during his time in New York, had been approached by General Clinton to accept a commission in the British Army but had turned it down. Considering his dire financial condition, which had only gotten worse since his return to North America, this would indicate that he was loyal to the colonies.

After his rejection for commission in the Continental Army, he returned to New Hampshire where he learned his wife had filed for divorce. The divorce would become final in 1778 and the true basis for it has never been learned. Speculation is that Rogers' repeated absences from home and little or no financial support for his wife and son had much to do with it.

Rogers headed again for Philadelphia, apparently with the thought in mind of again offering his services. Sabine in his biographical sketch of Rogers, indicates that as early as January 1776, Washington had come to the conclusion that

Wheelock's letter was untrue as to Rogers being in Canada, but still felt that Rogers needed to be watched because of his much suspected unfriendly views to his native land. According to Sabine in June 1776, Washington wrote, "Upon information that Major Rogers was traveling through the country under suspicious circumstances I thought it necessary to have him secured. I therefore sent after him. He was taken at South Amboy (New Jersey), and to New York. Upon examination, he informed me that he came from New Hampshire, the country of his usual abode, where he had left his family; and pretended he was destined to Philadelphia on business with Congress.

As by his own confession, he had crossed Hudson's River at New Windsor and was taken so far out of his proper and direct route to Philadelphia, this consideration, added to the length of time he had taken to perform his journey, his being found in so suspicious a place as Amboy...."

It must be remembered that Rogers had been ordered out of New York by Lord Sterling. Never to return. New Windsor was above New York on the Hudson. From there it was a straight line to Amboy, then to Trenton and on into Philadelphia. For a trained surveyor, Washington apparently could not read a map.

It has been implied that Rogers felt if his last request for a commission in the Continental Army failed he could at least get permission to go to Florida and sail from there to England. He had nothing left to keep him in North America.

Rogers was put in jail and remained there while the Declaration of Independence was being signed. Again, realizing that his services were not wanted, he requested permission to go to the West Indies and sail from there to England. This was to be denied. It was either prison or escape. Sometime during the night of 8-9 July 1776, Rogers escaped from jail.

On 6 August 1776 General Howe reported to Lord Germain, "Major Rogers, having escaped to us from Philadelphia, is empowered to raise a battalion of Rangers, which, I hope, may be useful in the course of the campaign."

To raise recruits for the new unit, Rogers had a circular printed which promised in part that the recruits would receive "their proportion of all rebel lands." What he got was the scum of New York, etc., both in the officer corps and other ranks. The unit was so bad that the regular army wanted nothing to do with them. In October 1776 the "Queen's Rangers" were routed from a fortified position on Long Island and soundly beaten by Lord Sterling. Rogers escaped and began drinking quite heavily. This eventually led to his being relieved of his command.

In 1779, the British sent him and his brother James to Canada to recruit with dismal failure. Rogers was imprisoned in Halifax for unpaid debts and when finally released in January 1781, while aboard a ship for New York, he was taken prisoner by a Continental privateer and ended up in prison again, where he stayed until May 1782, when he was released and sailed with the evacuating British Army for England.

Back in England, Rogers fared no better. He was in and out of debtors' prison, had numerous assignments against his half pay, drank heavily, contracted what we know today as tuberculosis and sustained a bad head injury in a fall. The end came on 18 May 1795 in a room he rented from a John Walker of Southwark. He was buried two days later in a rainstorm in the church yard of St. Mary's Church in Newington, hard by the Elephant and Castle Inn. There were two unknown mourners.

His passing was noted in *The Morning Press*, "Lieutenant Colonel Rogers, who died on Thursday last in the Borough, served in America during the last war, in which he performed prodigious feats of valour. He was a man of uncommon strength, but a long confinement in the Rules of King's Bench, had reduced him to the most miserable state of wretchedness."

So ended an era.

Newington: St Mary's Church as seen from the southwest, circa 1800. Where Robert Rogers originally was buried.

Uniform Illustrations

by

Clyde A. Risley

The uniforms illustrated here were standard for the regular army. Independent companies varied by unit and state. Highland regiments wore kilts in the tartan of the individual who raised them. As an example, the Frasers wore the Fraser tartan. The exception was the Black Watch (42nd Foot) who wore a kilt specifically designed for them.

Grenadiers wore a mitre headdress, battalion companies wore a tricorn and light infantries wore a cropped down version of the tricorn, in some instances what was called a jockey's cap.

Coats and waistcoats were with rare exception red, as were trousers. Facings and lace on the uniform designated the unit. There were summer and winter uniforms as well as cold weather overcoats and head coverings. Gaiters, which were in use during the French and Indian War, were white, black or brown in color.

The 48th Foot had buff facings. The 44th had yellow facings. The 35th had orange facings and the 60th had royal blue. The 55th Foot (Lord Howe's regiement) wore a short brown coatee with no facings. The artillery wore a blue coat with red facings. Naval units wore dark blue and their officers, blue coats with white facings.

The French army wore white with facings varying by unit. The Canadian troops wore sky blue. French artillery wore the same color uniforms as the British. Canadian artillery wore all red.

Officer Rogers and the Rangers

Ranger on the move

Enlisted Ranger

His Majesty's Independent Company Of Rangers / 181

Grenadier, 48th Regiment of Foot

182 / Relief Is Greatly Wanted

60th Regiment of Foot

HIS MAJESTY'S INDEPENDENT COMPANY OF RANGERS /183

Light Infantry, 55th Regiment of Foot

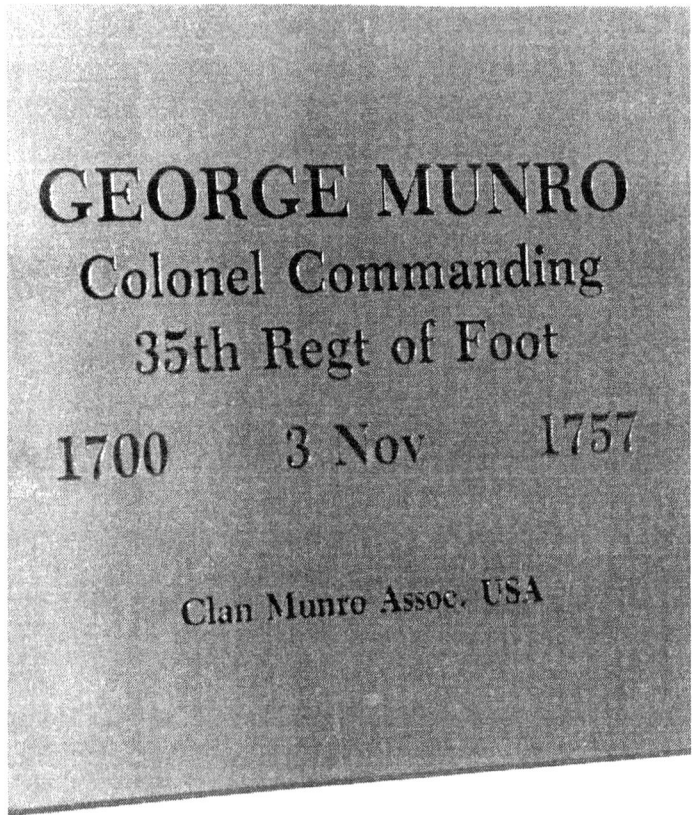

Grave marker for Lt. Col. George Monro at St. Peter's Episcopal Church, Albany, New York. The Army spelling of Munro was used. Clan spelling has been both Munro and Monro over the years, as has Monroe.

Participants in the ceremony to place the grave marker for Lt. Col. Monro in St. Peter's Episcopal Church on 4 November 1984. From left: Jack Monro, Rev. Dr. Laman H. Bruner, Jr., the author, Rev. Robert L. Zerbe, Clifford Andrews, William Monro. Photograph by James Hanley of Albany, N.Y.

About The Author

Ed Dodge's enthusiasm for French and Indian War history began during his childhood in the state of New York. Historical research has been his hobby for many years. He has written articles for the *Bulletin*, published by the Military History Society in England.

Dodge, a veteran of the Marine Corps and Air Force, learned of Lt. Col. Munro's gravesite through the Clan Munro Association, U.S.A. With their cooperation he was able to see that a marker was placed at the gravesite in the narthex of St. Peter's Episcopal Church, Albany, N.Y.

Relief is Greatly Wanted is the fruit of more than twenty years of research.

A retired insurance professional, Ed Dodge lives in Springfield, Illinois, with his wife, Ann.

Bibliography and Sources

Ainsworth, Major John F. *The Royal Sussex Regiment.* Derby, U.K.: English Life Publications, 1976.

America, Who Was Who. Chicago: Marquis Publishing, 1896.

Author, Y. Z. "Forts," *The Journal of the Society of Army Historical Research,* p. 215, Vol. 5, 1926.

Bain, Robert. *The Clans and Tartans of Scotland.* London & Glasgow: Collins Clear Type Press, 1954 Reprint.

Bisbee, Ernest E. *The Empire State Scrap Book.* Lancaster, N.H.: Bisbee Press, 1939.

Box, Arthur B. "Stinging Defeat Suffered," *Military History Magazine,* February 1993. Leesburg, Va: Cowles Enthusiast Media, History Group.

Boy Scouts of America. *Indian Lore Merit Badge Pamphlet.* North Brunswick, N.J.: Boy Scouts of America, 1959.

Connell, Brian. *The Savage Years.* Harper & Brothers, 1959.

Cuneo, John R. *Robert Rogers of the Rangers.* New York: Oxford University Press, 1950.

Dictionary of Canadian Biography. Vol. II, 1701 to 1740, pp. 565-574; Vol. III, 1741 to 1770, pp. 555-557; Vol. IV, 1771 to 1800, pp. 425-429, 512-514, 660-674. Toronto: University of Toronto Press.

Dictionary of National Biography, Vol. XVII. Robinson-Sheares. London: Oxford University Press, 1920.

Dodge, E. J. "Colonel Robert Rogers and the Natty Bumpo Connection." *The Bulletin, Vol. XXXX, #159.* Signland Ltd., Farmham, Surrey, UK: Military Historical Society, February 1990.

Dodge, E. J. "Six Days of Purgatory, One Day of Hell," *The Bulletin,* Vol. XXXVII, No. 146, November 1986; and Vol. XXXVII, No. 147, February 1987. Pictons, Chippenham, Wiltshire, U.K.: The Military Historical Society, 1987.

Dodge, Joseph T. *Dodge Family Genealogy, 1629-1896.* Madison, Wis.: Democrat Printing Co. 1898.

Encyclopedia Britannica. Chicago: University of Chicago Press, 1973.

Fazzini, Lillian Davids, with Dan Beard. *Indians of America.* Racine, WI: Whitman Pubishing Co., 1935.

Fergault, Guy. *Canada, The War of the Conquest.* Toronto, Canada: Oxford Press, 1969.

Gifford, Stanley M. *Fort William Henry 1755-1757, A History.* Pamphlet, 1955.

Hamilton, E. P. *The French and Indian War.* Garden City, N.Y.: Double Day Books, 1962.

Haswell, Major Jock. *The Queen's Regiment.* Regimental Committee, 1985.

Holbrook, Sabra. *The French Founders of North America and Their Heritage.* New York: Atheneum Press, 1976.

Ieckie, Robert. The Wars of America. Harper & Row, 1988.

Illustrated Columbia Encyclopedia, New York and London: Columbia University Press, 3rd ed., 1963.

Kahn, David. "Washington's New York Spy Network," *Great Battles Magazine,* September 1993. Leesburg, Va.: Cowles Enthusiast Media, History Group.

Kopperman, Paul E. "The British High Command and Soldiers' Wives in America, 1755-1783," *Journal of The Society for Army Historical Research,* Vol. LX, No. 241, Spring 1982. Chelsea, London: National Army Museum, Grillford, Ltd.

Laws, Lt. Col. (Retired) "R.N. and R.A. in Virginia, 1755," *Journal of The Society for Army Historical Research,* FR Hist. S., Vol. LVII, No. 232, Winter 1979.

Loescher, Burt Garfield. *The History of Rogers' Rangers, Vol. III, Officers and Non-Commissioned Officers.* London: National Army Museum, n.p., n.d.

Martineau, A.G. D. *History of The Royal Sussex Regiment.* Chichester, U.K.: Moore & Tillyer Ltd., 1953.

Meredith, Roy. *The American Wars, 1755-1953.* Cleveland & New York: World Publishing Co. 1955.

Montressor Journals. Edited by G. D. Scull. New York: New York State Historical Society Publication Fund Series, 1881.

Morris, Richard E. *Encyclopedia of American History.* Harper & Row, 1970.

National Cyclopedia of American Biography, Vol. I, pg. 87. Clifton, N.J.: J. T. White Publishing, 1892. Rev. 1937.

National Geographic Society. *Indians of the Americas.* Washington, D.C.: The National Geographic Society. 1955 Rev. 1965 7th ed.

New Century Cyclopedia of Names. Appleton, Century and Crofts.

O'Callaghan, E.B., and B. Fernow. *Muster Rolls of New York Provincial Troops, 1755-1764.* New York: New York State Historical Society Publication Fund Series, 1897.

Parade Magazine. "The Great Pennsylvania Fraud." p. 14, May 13, 1984.

Pell, S. H. P. "Fort Ticonderoga," *The Journal of The Society for Army Historical Research.* Vol. 7, 1928.

Peterson, Harold L. *Round Shot and Rammers.* New York: Bonanza Books, 1969.

Risley, Clyde A. and William F. Imrie. "Soldiers of The French and Indian War," *Military Modeler, 1978 Year Book.* Canoga Park, Ca.: Challenge Publications, 1978.

Robinson, Willard B. *American Forts, Architectural Form and Function.* Champaign: University of Illinois Press, 1977.

Sabine, Lorenzo. *Biographical Sketches of Loyalists of The American Revolution with an Historical Essay, Vol II.* Boston: Little Brown & Co., 1864.

Society of Antiquaries of Scotland, Proceedings. Vol. I, Fifth Series, Vol. II. Edinburgh, U.K.: Neill & Co. Ltd., 1916.

Strum, Harvey. "Stephen Cross and the Fall of Oswego," *The Bulletin*, Vol. XXXVI, No. 143, The Military Historical Society, 1986.

Tebbel, John. *The Compact History of The Indian Wars.* New York: Hawthorn Books, 1966.

Trimen, Richard. *Historical Memoir of the 35th Royal Sussex Regiment of Foot.* Southampton, U.K.: The Southampton Times Newspaper and Printing and Publishing Co., Ltd., 1873.

Wellman, Paul I. *Indian Wars and Warriors East.* Boston: Houghton Mifflin Publishing, 1959.

Wentzel, Alice S. "Spy's Literary Role," *Military History Magazine,* June 1990. Leesburg, Va: Cowles Enthusiast Media, History Group.

Microfilm:

MC 11, Colonial Office, Series CO 5, Original Correspondence, Vol. 48, pp. 179-181, Microfilm Reel B-2112, National Archives of Canada, Public Programs Branch.

MIG 13, W.O. 1, Vol. 1, folios 122-123; Microfilm Reel B 3059, National Archives of Canada, Historical Resources Branch.

MG 5, B. 1, Vol. 10, pp. 368-376; Microfilm Reel C-12, 570, National Archives of Canada, Historical Resources Branch.

Libraries, Museums, and Public Records Offices:

Huntington Library, San Marino, California. *Loudon Collection - Americana; French and Indian War Archives.* Department of Manuscripts.

Public Records Office, Dublin, Ireland, 1985.

Supreme Court, Dublin 7, Dublin Ireland.

VCH Survey, p. 72, London: 1912.

INDEX

17TH Regiment of Foot, 128
26TH Regiment of Foot, Cameronians, 115
35TH Regiment of Foot, 2 52 55 64 67 78 97 100 104 109 114 116-117
42ND Regiment of Foot (Black Watch), 125
44TH Regiment of Foot, 2 19 31 45 52
48TH Regiment of Foot, 39 52 55
60TH Regiment of Foot, 2 50 97 101 128 (Royal Americans) 55
62ND Regiment of Foot, 101
80TH Light Infantry 163
ABBOTT, Jacob 163
ABENAKI INDIANS, 50 162 Of Panaonaniski In Acadia 108 Rogers' Dislike For 165
ABERCROMBIE, Gen 101 133
ABERCROMBY, James "Mrs Nabby Crombie" 125
ACADIA, 51
ACADIANS, 16
ADIRONDACKS, 1
ALBANY, 11 21 24 47 93 97 100 115 132 148 150-152 157 172
ALGONQUIN INDIANS, 6-7 50
ALLEN, Ethan, Career Of 146
AMHERST, Jeffrey 101 116 125 127 Career Of 127-128
AMHERST COLLEGE, Massachusetts 128

ANDIATAROCTE, 2
ANGEL, Col 57 82 84
APPALACHIANS, 9-10
ARIKARA INDIANS, 50
ARNOLD, Benedict 36 132 146-147 150 154-155 And Gates' Jealousy 152
ARTILLERY, British Complimented By French 98 Burst 69-70 72 Deemed Necessary At Fort William Henry 83
ARTILLERY COVE, Enemy Landing Point 60
ASHLAND, Wisconsin 51
ASSINIBOIA INDIANS, 50
AUCHINBOWIE, Scotland 116
BAIRD, Sandy 101
BAMFORD, Wm 104
BARTMAN, G (Webb's Aide De Camp) 57 67-68
BARTZ, 150
BASTILLE, 37
BATEAUX, 32
BAYBOATS, 44
BEARN, 81 Battalion 50 Regiment To Form Part Of Escort From Fort William Henry 79
BEAUJEU, 17 Daniel-Hyacinthe-Marie Lienard De 16
BELFAST, Regiment 116
BEMIS HEIGHTS, 152
BENNINGTON, Vermont 151 Battle Of 127 John Stark At 45

BLACK WATCH, (42nd Regiment Of Foot) 125
BLANCHARD, Joseph 24
BLANCHARD'S RANGERS, New Hampshire 165
BLOOD, Human, Drinking Of 113
BLOODY MORNING SCOUT, 27 133
BLOODY POND, 25 133 155
BOLTON'S LANDING, 84
BOONE, Daniel 17
BOSTON, 145 151 154 158 173
BOUGAINVILLE, Louis Antoine De 93 Journals 94
BOURLAMAQUE, Monsieur De 93
BOY SCOUTS OF AMERICA, Explorer Program 161
BRADDOCK, Edward 13 14 19 24 28 87 Death Of 16 His Mistress Killed 16
BRADDOCK'S DEFEAT, Described In Spendelow's Journal 13-16
BRADSTREET, John 129
BRANDY, 56
BRANDYWINE, 148 158
BRANT, Joseph, Mohawk War Chief 27 156 Career Of 156-157 Death Of 157
BRANT, Molly 27 156
BROWN, Elizabeth 166 Ens 80 Jacob 171 John 171 Private 87 Thomas 47
BROWN BESS MUSKETS, 32
BRUCE, Margaret 115
BUNKER HILL, 151 154 John Stark At 44 Putnam At 100
BURGOYNE, John 127 148 151-152 154-155 A Playwright 154

BURGOYNE, John (cont.) Career Of 154 Death Of 154 Defeat 154 Surrender At Saratoga 45
BURGOYNE'S HYENAS, 126 151
BURKE, Edmund 127
BURTON, R 17 55
BUTLER, 158 John 156 John, Career Of 156 Walter 156
BUTLER'S RANGERS, 156
CAMBRIDGE, Massachusetts 146
CAMDEN, Gates Defeated At 155
CAMERONIANS, 115
CAMPBELL, John 126
CANADA, Internal Politics 6
CANAJOHARIE, 155
CANNON, 32 At Fort William Henry 31 Burst From Overuse 62 65 One Piece Granted In Capitulation 76
CAPITULATION, 74 107 Articles Of 75-77
CAPTURE, By French And Indians 87-88
CARILLON, 50 80 86 100 112 125 Abercromby's Assault On 125-126 See also Ticonderoga
CARLETON, British Gen 173 Sir Guy, Gov Of Canada 127 147 148 154
CARLSON, R 13
CAROLINA PLANTATIONS, 125
CAROLINAS, 155 172
CARPENTERS, at Fort William Henry 14
CARVER, 90-91 165 170 James 131 Jonathan 131

Index / 195

CASUALTIES, French, Estimated 97 Indian, No Count Ever Given 98 Varying Figures 95
CAUGHNAWAGA INDIANS, 50
CAYUGA INDIANS, 50
CHAMPLAIN, 7 Samuel De 6
CHECKAUNKUM, Mohigan Ranger 162
CHERRY VALLEY RAID, 156 157
CHESTER COUNTY, Pennsylvania 147
CHINGACHGOOK, 162
CHIPPEWA INDIANS, 50
CHOISEUL ISLANDS, 94
CHRUCKSHANKS, Chas 104
CLAN MONRO, Scotland 113
CLINTON, DeWitt 155 George 155 James 155 157-158 173 James Career Of 155 James Death Of 155
CLONFIN, County Longford Ireland 115
COLLINS, Mr, British Artillery Commander 72
COLONISTS, Dutch 7 English 7
CONCORD, New Hampshire 165
CONNECTICUT, 36 Forces 68
CONTINENTAL CONGRESS, 172 John Sullivan In 158 St Clair In 149
COOPER, James Fenimore 2 161 162 171
CORNPLANTER, Seneca War Chief, 156 157 Death Of 157
COUREURS DE BOIS, 7 16 50 62 81 83 French Lack Of Control Over 94

COURT MARTIAL, Of Massachusetts Lieutenant 85
CREEK INDIANS, 50
CREES, And Sioux, Peace Treaty Negotiated By Joseph Marin 51
CREVE COUER, Fort At 9
CROSBY, Enoch 171-172
CROWN POINT, 81 132-133 147 164 127 See also Fort St Frederic
CUNEO, John R 131 161
CUNNINGHAM, Capt 67 Lady Mary 101
D'AFFREY, Monsieur Le Count 107
DARBY'S RANGERS, 161
DARTMOUTH COLLEGE, 156 172
DECLARATION OF INDEPENDENCE, 174
DEERFIELD, Massachusetts 5 Raid 9
DEFIANCE, Mt 148
DEGANAWIDAH, Iroquois Prophet 149
DELAWARE INDIANS, 11 13 50 Cheated Out Of Their Land In 1737 10
DENONVILLE, Marquis De 7
DESERTERS, 83 German, From Fort Carillon 80 Of Montcalm At Fort William Henry 85
DETROIT, 129 145 166 Putnam At 100
DIAMOND ISLAND, 40
DIESKAU, Baron Von 19 21 24 25 (sic, Diskeau) 112
DIETZ, 150
DODGE, Jonathan 163 Josiah 163 Caleb 163

DONEGAL, Earl Of 116
DRIVING TOUR, 133
DUMAS, Jean-Daniel 16
DUNKELD, Battle Of 115
DUTCH, Colonists 7
EAGLES, Glen 101
EASTMAN, Ebenezer 165
ELEPHANT AND CASTLE INN, 175
ENGLAND, 174-175
ENGLISH, Approach To Dealing With Indians 10 Colonists 7
ERIE INDIANS, 50
EUROPE, Power Struggles Contributed To War In North America 1
EXPLORERS, French 9
EYRE, William 19 31 40 44 45 Later Years And Death 45
FAESCH, Rudolphus 109 111-112
FALKLANDS, 94
FALLEN TIMBERS, Battle Of 147
FERGUSON, ---- 132
FIGHTING DEACON, Capt Hobbs 32 39
FIREARMS, Trade Between English And Iroquois 7
FISHKILL, New York 172
FLESH, Human, Eating Of 113
FLETCHER, Maj 57 82 84
FLORIDA, 174
FOLSOM, Capt 24-25
FORBES, John 128 Death Of 129
FORT ANNE, 36 133 145 148 Anne Remains Of 82
FORT CARILLON, 37 82 127 Inventory Of Captured Munitions 104 See also Ticonderoga
FORT CLINTON, 5 11 21 36 LaCorne At Fall Of 126 Putnam At 100
FORT DUQUESNE, 11 13-14 93 128
FORT EDWARD, 19 21 24 27 32 37 52-53 56-59 61 80-82 84-87 89 92-93 99-100 102-103 108 132-133 145 151-152 154 164 166 Defenses Being Bolstered 59 Escort Sent Out To Fort William Henry 85 Headquarters Of Rangers 163 Shots Could Be Heard From Fort William Henry 85
FORT FRONTENAC, 11 129
FORT GEORGE, 27-28 107 145-147 155
FORT LYDIUS, 19
FORT LYMAN, 27
FORT MONTGOMERY Putnam At 100
FORT NECESSITY, 12
FORT NIAGARA, 11 52 129 156
FORT ONTARIO, 27-28
FORT OSWEGO, 16 27-28 79
FORT ST FREDERIC, 19 21 37 164
FORT ST JEAN, 37
FORT STANWIX 104 149-150 Treaty Of 157-158
FORT TICONDEROGA, 132-133 145-148 St Claire Commander Of, In 1777 149 See also Ticonderoga
FORT WILLIAM HENRY, 2 19 21 24 28 36-37 41 44-45 48 50 52-53 58-60 77 81-82 93 95 99 102-104 107 110-111 115-117 131-133 145 163-164

FORT WILLIAM HENRY, (cont.)
Construction And Armament 31 Navy At 32 Points Of Vulnerability 32 St Patrick's Day Attack 38-40 47 1000 Men And Some Artillery Dispatched To 83 1000 Men Dispatched From Fort Edward On 2 Or 3 Aug 59 And Camp Layout Of 86 Artillery Deemed Necessary 83 Bastions Needed To Be Raised 83 Battle As Previously Told 61-63 Battle Aug 3 4 And 5 64 Battle Early Casualties 67 Battle Facts 63-65 86 Battle Skirmishing 64 Bombardment From Two Sides 61 Breaching Of The Weakened Spot 61 British Artillery Barrage 64 Camp 31 86 95 Damage During Siege 74 Defense Measures Determined By Council Of War 59 Defensive Measures 83 Early Casualties 64 Fired Upon By Boats 84 Interior Damage To Northwest Bastion 65 Massacre 63 Problems Caused By Construction And Uncleanness 55 Smoke Could Be Seen From Fort Edward 85
FOSTER, Levi 171
FOX INDIANS, 50
FRASER, Hugh 152 154
FRASER'S HIGHLANDERS, 52
FRENCH, Approach To Dealing With Indians 10

FRENCH, (cont.)
Forces Came By Boat And Over Land 86 Reports Misleading 85
FRYE, Joseph 85 91-92 104
FUR TRADE, 6
FUR TRADERS, 16
GAGE, Thomas 17 154 163 166 170
GARDINER, Luke 104
GATES, Horatio 17 152 Death Of 155 Horatio Career Of 154 Jealousy Of Benedict Arnold 152 Rival Of Washington 155
GAUCHER, Sieur 112
GEORGE, King Of England 148
GERMAIN, Lord 148 174
GERMAN FLATS, 150
GERMAN DRAGOONS, 151
GERMANTOWN, 158
GERMAN TROOPS, 152
GHENT, Peace Treaty Of 129
GIBRALTAR, 13
GILMAN, John 104
GLAZIER, Col 57 82 84
GLENS FALLS, New York, Supply Train Ambushed Near 126
GOOD, Lt 64
GORDON, Harry 14 17 57 82 84
GOSSE (GOFFE), John 104
GRANT, James 128
GREAT CARRYING PLACE, 19
GREAT LAKES, Region Explored By French 9
GREEN BAY, Wisconsin 51
GREEN MOUNTAIN BOYS, 146
GRENADIERS, 14

GROG, 56 Supply Cut Off By Stark On St Patrick's Day 39
GUIENNE, Battalion 50
GUNDOLAS, 44
HAIR, Lord 101
HALFWAY HOUSE, Tavern On Military Road 59 83
HALIFAX, 109 175
HAMILTON, E P 131 Will 104
HARBE, Monsieur 112
HARD-TACK, 56
HERKIMER, Nicholas 149 Career Of 150 Death Of 150
HOBBS, Humphrey (the Fighting Deacon) 32 39 Death By Smallpox 47
HOLLAND, 101
HOME, Lord 101
HOOSICK, 11
HORICAN, 2
HOSTAGE, To Be Given 76
HOWE, Earl Admiral Richard 125
HOWE, Gen William 125 132 174
HOWE, Viscount Brigadier George Augustus Lord 125 148 151 Buried Next To Monro In Albany 126 Death Of 126 125
HUBBARD, Thomas 92
HUBBARDTON, 145
HUDSON HIGHLANDS, Putnam At 100
HUDSON RIVER, 19 148 163 174
HUDSON RIVER VALLEY, 36 155
HUDSON'S BAY, 5
HURON INDIANS, 2 11 19 21 32 36 39 47 50-51 62 80-81 85 90 100 116 162

HURON INDIANS, (cont.) Attack Fort William Henry 61 Attack On Schenectady 8 Devastated By Iroquois 7 Devious Plan Of 79
ILLINOIS INDIANS, 9 50
ILLINOIS RIVER, 9
INCE, Chas 104
INDIA, 170
INDIANS, French Lack Of Control Over 94 Plunder And Murder After The Siege 77 89 Still A Problem After The War 145
INFANTRY, Montcalm's 62
INQUIRY, Board Of 58
IOWA INDIANS, 50
IRELAND, Burgoyne Appointed Commander In Chief Of 154
IROQUOIS, 2 6 9 151 158 Attack On LaChine In 1688 7 Desert British And Ally With The French 45 Hatred For The French 7
IROQUOIS, Confederation 27
JACOBS, Capt 162 Capt The Elder 162-163
JAIL, Rogers' Escape From 174
JEFFERSON, Thomas 149
JERSEY REGIMENT, 104
JOHNSON, Guy 155-156 Career Of 156 Death Of 156
JOHNSON, Sir John 155-156 Career Of 155
JOHNSON, Molly 156
JOHNSON, Sir William 2 19 21 24 25 27 79 81 70 85 129 155-156 166
JOHNSTOWN, 155
JOLIET, 9
KICKAPOO INDIANS, 50
KILBY, James 93 95 97 113

Index / 199

KILBY, James (cont.)
    Description Of Siege
    Aftermath 77 Report Of 63
    Account Of Massacre 92
    Account Of Provisions
    Captured By French 104
KILLED WOUNDED AND
    MISSING REPORT 97
KING HENDRICK, 24 27
KINGSBRIDGE, New York 172
LA CHINE, Attacked By
    Iroquois In 1688 7
LA CORNE, 86 And Pontiac's
    Uprising 127 Blamed For
    Desertion Of Indians At
    Battle Of Saratoga 127
    Career Of 126-127 Death Of
    127 In Charge Of Burgoyne's
    Hyenas 127 In Command Of
    Blockade Of Military Road
    126 In Shipwreck 126
    Indian Slave Owner 126
    Officer Of French Escort 126
LA CROS, Sieur 112
LAC ST SACREMENT, 2 111
LADD, Daniel 165
LA FAYETTE, Marquis De 171
LAKE CHAMPLAIN, Lake 2
    16 19 36 80 133 147-148
    163-164
LAKE GEORGE, 1-2 19 21 24-
    25 36 40 47 50 84 86 103
    117 133 163 Battle Of, 21
    24-25 27 Boats Planked
    Together And Carrying
    Cannon 83
LAKE ONTARIO, 11-12 27
    129
LANGUEDOC, 81 Battalion
    50 Regiment To Form Part
    Of Escort From Fort
    William Henry 79
LA PRAIRIE, Nova Scotia 8

LA REINE, Battalion 50
LA SALLE, 9
LA SARRE, 81 Battalion 50
LEATHERSTOCKING TALES,
    (books) 161
LEBANON, Connecticut 156
LENNOX, Maj John 126
LETTER, Captured From
    Courier 65 From Monro To
    Montcalm 65 Intercepted 68
    71
LETTERS, Between Monro
    And Webb 65-73
LEVI, Sutler 40
LEVIS, 82 86 93 Career And
    Death 50 Francois Gaston
    Duc De 50 Marquis De 37
    61 86
LIQUOR, And Indians After
    Siege 108 110 Destroyed By
    Monro After Capitulation
    107
LONDON, Young At 101
LONDONDERRY, New
    Hampshire 39
LONG ISLAND, 175 Battle Of
    158 Putnam At 100
LONGUEIL, 112
LOUDON, 107 Earl Of 44 113
    Lord 40 47 55 57-58 101-102
    104 106 125
LOUISBOURG, 51 116 127
    164
LOUISIANA, 11 37
LOYALISTS, 149
LYMAN, Phineas 19 25 27 57
    80-81 82 84
MACKINAW CITY, Michigan,
    Explored By Joseph Marin
    51
MACLEOD, 85 William 55
MALARIA, 172

MARIN DE LA MALGUE, Joseph 51 81 126 Against Rogers Rangers 52 And Destruction Of Fort Clinton 52 Attack On Woodcutters At Fort Edward 51 Career Of 51-52 Death In Madagascar 52 French Version Of Robert Rogers 51 Imprisoned Twice 52 Saved Putnam From Death 100 Paul 51

MARINES, 81 French, To Form Part Of Escort From Fort William Henry 79

MARLBORO, New York 172

MARQUETTE, 9

MARTINIQUE, 154

MARYLAND, 36 52 170 172

MASONS, 171

MASSACHUSETTS, 132 166 Regiment 104 Regiment Near A State Of Mutiny 62 Salem 99

MASSACRE, At Fort William Henry 80 Attempted Coverup by French 113 Described In Frye's Diary 91

MCBRIDE, Eleanor 132 Joseph 132

MCCREA, Jane, Killing Of 151

MCFATRIDGE, Mary 165

MCGINNIS, Capt 24-25 81 163

MEDFORD, Massachusetts 173

MENOMINEE INDIANS, Warriors With Joseph Marin 51

MERCER, Col 28 Col James 27

MERCIER, Lt Col Francois Le 42 45 French Artillery Commander 72

MESSENGER, Between Webb And Monro Captured 62

METHUEN, Massachusetts 165

MIAMI INDIANS, 50

MICHILLIMACKINAC, 129 170 Rogers Governor Of 166

MICMAS INDIANS, 50

MIDDLEBURG, 155

MILITARY ROAD, 133

MILITIA, 2 89 Canadian 50 151 Col Parker's New Jersey 82 Colonial 51 Criticized By Monro 78 Disdain For Discipline At Fort William Henry 55 French Control Over 94 From Albany And Schenectady 85 Hampshire 56 78 163 Jersey 56 78 Massachusetts 28 56 78 85 91 New Hampshire 24 New Hampshire Captured And Killed 91 95 New Jersey 50-51 149 New York 24 145 150 Officers And Privates Killed During Siege 95 Pennsylvania 147

MINGO INDIANS, 50

MINNESOTA, 165 Indians From 50

MINOMINEE INDIANS, 50

MISKAYUNA, New York 115

MISSISSIPPI, Watershed Expedition 170

MISSISSIPPI RIVER, Explored By French 9

MISSOURI RIVER, Joseph Marin Searched For Western Sea Connection 51

MOHAWK INDIANS, 11 Five Villages Wiped Out By French In 1693 9 24-25 27 50 81 85 157 162

MOHAWK INDIANS, (cont.)
  From Canada 149
MOHAWK RIVER, 149
MOHAWK RIVER VALLEY, 11
  27 36 148 155-156
MOHIGAN INDIANS, 50
  Stockbridge 162 165
MONK, Capt 101
MONONGAHELA RIVER, 14
MONRO, Alexander 115
MONRO, Clan Of Scotland
  113
MONRO, George 52 55 57 59
  63-64 77 82 84 95 97 100
  101 103 106 110 113 115
  116 126 132 Asked For
  Assistance From Webb Aug
  4 83 Burial In Albany 115
  Career Of 115 Death Of
  114-115 Declines
  Montcalm's Surrender
  Terms 62 Disdain For
  Provincials And Praise For
  Regulars 78 Letters To
  Loudon 106 Memorial
  Plaque Placed 116 Petition
  For Retirement As A
  Physician 114 Reply To
  Montcalm 64 Report Of
  Captured Munitions 104
  See also Munro
MONRO, Jane 116
MONRO, John 116
MONRO, Margaret 115
MONRO, Sackville 116
MONROE, 116 Keith 115
MONTAGNAIS INDIANS, 50
MONTCALM, 21 28 37 47-48
  50 52 57 61 66 77 78 80-82
  85-86 93-94 103 106-110
  112-113 115 125 Advised
  British To Stay Overnight
  At Fort 79

MONTCALM, (cont.)
  Death Of 48 127 129 Offers
  Monro Surrender Terms 62
  Orders British To March
  Out At Midnight 79 Report
  Of Captured Munitions 104-
  105 Text Of Request To
  Monro To Surrender 63-64
MONTCALM-GOZON, Louis
  Joseph De-Marquis De
  Saint-Veran 48
MONTCALM AND WOLFE,
  (book) 127
MONTGOMERY, Richard 147
  Career Of 147 Death Of 147
MONTGOMERY'S
  HIGHLANDERS, 128
MONTREAL, 16 19 28 36-37
  40 44 50-51 93 95 100 109
  127 147 155 170 Attacked
  By Iroquois In 1691 8 Fall
  Of 129
MONTRESSOR, 55 57 59 82-
  83-85 87 James Gabriel,
  Journal Of 59 80 Account Of
  Arrival Of Survivors At Fort
  Edward 100
MONTREUIL, Chevalier De
  93
MORGAN, Daniel 152 154
  155
MORNING PRESS, 175
MORRIS, Brigade Major 57
MORTARS, At Fort William
  Henry 31-32 Burst 64
MUNRO, 89 91 93-94 116 See
  also Monro
NAMUR, Siege 115
NARRAGANSETT INDIANS,
  50 Tribe 11
NASCOPI INDIANS, 50
NAUNAUPTAUNK, 163
  Mohigan Ranger 162

NAVY, At Fort William Henry 32
NEGRO SERVANT, Monro's 93
NEGROES, 89 91
NEW FRANCE, See Canada
NEW HAMPSHIRE, 131-132 158 166 172-173 Regiment 104
NEW HEBRIDES, 94
NEW JERSEY, 101 155
NEW LONDON, Connecticut 156
NEW ORLEANS, 9
NEW WINDSOR, 174
NEW YORK, 146 155-156 158 166 173-175 Spy Network In 172 Young At 101
NEW YORK CITY, 147-148 172
NEWPORT, Rhode Island 158
NIAGARA FRONTIER, 36
NIPMUCK INDIANS, 50
NORTH, Lord 171
NORTHWEST PASSAGE, (book) 87 161
NORTHWEST PASSAGE, Rogers' Search For 166 170
NORTHWEST TERRITORY, St Claire First Governor Of 149
NOVA SCOTIA, 116
OGDEN, Jonathan 53 66 104
OHIO (RIVER) WATERSHED, 11 13
OHIO RIVER, 81 Explored By French 9
OHIO TERRITORY, 147
OHIO VALLEY, 93
OJIBWAY INDIANS, 50 And Peace With Sioux 51
ONEIDA INDIANS, 50 149 157

ONONDAGA INDIANS, 50
ORANGE COUNTY, New York 155
"ORANGES", 116
ORD, Capt 57 82 84
ORISKANY, 151 155-157 Battle Of 149
ORISKANY CREEK, 150
ORMSBY, Capt 64 109
OSWEGO, 19 81 93 166
OSWEGO RIVER, 27
OTTAWA INDIANS, 50
OTWAYS, Grenadier Company 79 Regiment (35th) 84 115 116
PARIS, 37
PARKER, John 50-51 82 104 111 Ambush Of 60
PARKMAN, Francis 127 131
PAULING, New York 172
PENN, Thomas 10 William 10
PENNSYLVANIA, 36 52 101 149
PENOBSCOT INDIANS, 50
PEQUOT INDIANS, 11 50 Uncas 162
PERTHSHIRE, 115
PHILADELPHIA, 128-129 172-174 Young At 101
PHILLIPS, Artillery Commander 148
PITT, 128
PITTSBOROUGH, 128
PITTSBURGH, 11
PLYMOUTH COLONY, 11
"PONTEACH", Play Written By Robert Rogers 166
PONTIAC'S REBELLION, 145 155-156 166
PORINE, Lord 101
PORTAGE, 133
PORT ROYAL, Nova Scotia 5 8

POTAWATOMIE INDIANS, 50
POTTER, Nathaniel 170
PRIMROSE, Lord 101
PRINCETON, 158 John Stark At 44
PRISONERS, 41 44 47 93 95 97 Return Of, To Carillon 112 Taken From Indians By Montcalm And Sent To Louisbourg 109 Thinly Veiled Threats Regarding 113 Capitulation Terms 76
PROVISIONS, At Fort William Henry 56
PUTNAM, 53 59 60 80 82 83 85 99 Israel Captured By Hurons 100 In Revolution 100 Ranger Officer Rescued From Hurons By Joseph Marin 51
PUTNAM'S RANGERS, 67
QUEBEC, 37 48 51 147 Battle Of 116 Campaign, John Stark At 45 155 Fall Of 127 129
QUEEN'S RANGERS, 175
QUEEN'S REGIMENT, 116-117
"RABBLE IN ARMS", 154
RANGER ISLAND, 163
RANGERS, 32 36 39-40 42 44 52-53 56 60 66 68 70 80 81 83 85 87 97 99-100 104 106 125 128 161-166 171 174 Blanchard's 165 Darby's 161 His Majesty's Independent Company Of 2 Of The US Army 161 Putnam's 67 Queen's 175 Rogers' 25,67,145 Scouting At Sabbath Day Point 60 Uniform 162 164

RANGERS, (cont.) Weapons Of 164
RECHELLE, De La 107
REGULARS, French Control Over 94
REIDESEL, Baron 152
REPORTS, Conflicting 84
REVOLUTION (American), 149 154 156 158 171 John Stark's Service In 44 St Claire In 149
RIVINGTON, James 172
ROBERT ROGERS OF THE RANGERS, (book) 161
ROBERTS, Benjamin 170 Kenneth 87 131 161 163
ROGERS, Arthur 173
ROGERS, Elizabeth 166 170 173
ROGERS, James 170 175 James Sr 165
ROGERS, Mary 165
ROGERS, Richard 52 Richard Death From Smallpox 53
ROGERS, Robert 25 39 52 81 93 128 131 161-162 164 47 Burial Of 132 Career Of 165-166 170-175 Death Of 175 Divorce 173 99 166 171-175 Financial Problems Of 166 Imprisoned For Treason 170 Imprisoned In Canada 175 Imprisoned In England 170 Play Written By 166
ROGERS ISLAND, 163
ROGERS RANGERS, 25 67 145
ROME, New York 104
ROUBAUD, Description Of Murder Scene 78 Father Pierre Saved The Lives Of Woman And Child 90

ROYAL AMERICANS, 55 101 109 113 See also 60th Regiment Of Foot
ROYAL ARTILLERY, 97 104
ROYAL ROUSSILLON, Battalion 50 81 116
ROYAL SUSSEX Regiment, 115 116-117
RUM, 56
SABBATH DAY POINT, 82 Enemy Encampment 60 Parker's Patrol Ambushed 50
SABINE, 174 Lorenzo 171
SAILORS, 13 Considered Finest Gunners In The World 72
ST CLAIR, Sir John 17
ST CLAIRE, Arthur 149 Career Of 149 Court Martialed 149 Died Impoverished 149 Maj Gen Arthur 148
ST FRANCIS Abenaki Village Rogers Raid On 128 131 161
ST JAMES, Westminster London 80
ST LAWRENCE RIVER, 9 16 36 48 148 164
ST LEGER, Barry 148 150-151 155
ST LOUIS, 9
ST MARY'S NEWINGTON, Church Where Rogers Was Buried 175
ST PETER'S, Church 126 132
SALK INDIANS, 50
SALTONSTALL, Capt Richard 64 104
SALT PORK, 56
SAMOA, 94
SARATOGA, 21 36 152 154-155 Battle Of 127 Burgoyne's Surrender At 45

SARATOGA SPRINGS, 5 9 11
SASSACUS, Sachem Of The Pequot 162
SCALPING, 11, 87
SCHENECTADY, 21 French And Indian Attack In 1690 8
SCHOHARIE VALLEY, 155
SCHUYLER, Peter 9 11 Yost 150-151
SCHUYLER PATENT, 9 11 21
SCHUYLERVILLE, 151-152
SCOTLAND, 101 125
SCOWS, 32 44
SENECA INDIANS, 50 149 157 Tribe Attacked By Denonville 7
SHAWANOIES, Indains 50
SHAWNEE INDIANS, 50
SHIRLEY, Gov 166
SHUCKBURY, Richard 133
SICK AND WOUNDED, Killed 77 89 95 To Remain At Fort 76
SINCLAIR, Lord 101
SIOUX, Peace And Trade Agreements Made By Joseph Marin 51 Subtribes 50
SIX NATIONS, 149
SLOOPS, 32 Burned By French At Fort William Henry 43
SMALLPOX, 63 93 117 127 At Fort William Henry 55
SMITH, John 171
SOLOMON ISLANDS, 94
SOMERSWORTH, New Hampshire 157
SONS OF LIBERTY, 145-146 171
SOUTH AMBOY, New Jersey 174
SOUTH BAY, 81 133 Lake Champlain 80
SOUTH CAROLINA, 101 166

SOUTHWARK, 175
SPARKMAN, Thomas 39
SPEAKMAN, Thomas 32 39
SPENDELOW, Charles 13 17 87
SPIKEMAN, 47 53 Death Of 47 Thomas 39
STANWIX, John 101 104
STARK, John 32 39 40 99 125 132 151 Later Years 44 Made To Run The Gauntlet 39
STARVED ROCK, 9
STERLING, William Alexander, Lord 173 175
SULLIVAN, John 155 157 173 Career Of 157
SUPPLIES, Depleted 74
SURVIVORS, Remainder Arrived At Fort Edward 85
SUTLERS, Women As 56
SWIVELS, 32
SWORDS COUNTY, Ireland 147
SYMER, William 163
TAESCH, R 104
TAHITI, 94
TALLMADGE, Benjamin 172
TEYNHAM, Kent, England 80
THAYENDANEGA, 156
THE SPY, (book) 171
THURSON, Caithness Co Scotland 149
TICONDEROGA, 9 42 51 100 132 155 See also Carillon
TIYANOGA, See King Hendrick
TORIES, 150 155 156
"TOWN DESTROYER", The 157 (George Washington)
TOWNSEND, Robert 172
TRACY, Spencer, As Robert Rogers 161
TRENTON, 158 174

TRENTON, (cont.) John Stark At 44
TRICE, Capt 79
TRINITY COLLEGE, Dublin 147
TROIS-RIVIERES, 37 40 147 Attacked By Iroquois In 1691 8
TUSCARORA INDIANS, 50 149
TUTE, J 170
UNCAS, 162
VALCOUR ISLAND, Battle Of 147
VAUDREUIL, Francois-Pierre De Rigaud De 37 39 40 45 47-48 77 107-109 113 Gov Of Canada 19 37
VAUDREUIL, Rigaud 37 40 42 93 126 Rigaud Later Years 44
VEGETABLES, 56
VERMONT, 145
VIRGINIA, 36 128
WALKER, John 175
WALKING PURCHASE, 11
WAMPANOAG INDIANS, 50
WAR, Declared On France By England In 1756 36
WAR, French And Indian 5 Reasons For 6
WAR, Honors Of 77
WAR, King Georges 5 21 25 36 39-40 99 126 165
WAR, King Phillip's 10
WAR, King William's 5
WAR, Narragansett 10
WAR, Of Independence 128
WAR, Of The Austrian Succession 5 48 50 127
WAR, Of The Grand Alliance 5
WAR, Of The Polish Succession 48

WAR, Of The Spanish Succession 5 116
WAR, Pequot 10
WAR, Queen Anne's 5
WAR, Revolutionary 158
WAR, Seven Years' 5 127
WAR, Tribal 7
WASHINGTON, George 5 12-13 17 36 148 171-174 Ordered Punitive Expeditions Against Iroquois 157
WATER, 56
WAYNE, "Mad" Anthony 147 Career Of 147 Death Of 147
WEBB, Daniel 57 59-60 80 82-85 93 99 101-103 106 107 110 Advised Of Capitulation 85 At Fort William Henry In July 1757 56 Informed Of Attack On 4 Aug 83 Put In Command Of Lake George District 47 Suffered From Hypochondria 47
WEST INDIES, 174
WEST VIRGINIA, 154
WHALEBOATS, 32 50 82
WHEELOCK, Eleazar 156 172-174
WHITEHALL, 133 145 148
WHITE PLAINS, New York 172
WHITING, Nathaniel 24
WILLIAM III, King 116
WILLIAMS, Ephraim 19 24-25 Surgeon 24
WILLIAMS COLLEGE, 25
WILLIAMSON, 57 Adam 74
WILLIAMSTOWN, Massachusetts 25
WINNEBAGO INDIANS, 50
WISCONSIN, 165 Indians From 50
WISCONSIN RIVER, 51
WITHERINGTON, Ens 64
WOLFE, James, Death Of 127 Death Of 129 Description Of Northern New York And Canada 127
WOMEN, 13 As Sutlers 56 At Fort William Henry Duties Pay And Shelter 56
WOMEN AND CHILDREN 62 At Fort William Henry In August 1757 55 Killed At Burgoyne's Defeat 151 Killed At Fort William Henry 95 Murdered By Indians 90 No Count Given 97 With Burgoyne's Army 152
WOOD CREEK, 21 36 57 82 133
WOODCUTTERS, Attacked 82
WOODHULL, Abraham 172
WYOMING VALLEY, 156 Raid 157
"YANKEE DOODLE", 133
YORKTOWN, 155
YOUNG, John 55 57 59 67 69 74 83 104 109 112 Career Of 101 Letters Of 102-103 Wounds Of 100
YOUNG PRETENDER, 101

www.ingramcontent.com/pod-product-compliance
Lightning Source LLC
Chambersburg PA
CBHW071715160426
43195CB00012B/1684